Choices

The True Story of One Family's
Daring Escape to Freedom

D0813379

This is a remarkable and engaging true story of courage, hope, and perseverance.

In 1956, your parents, myself, and many other survivors around the world, were just barely healing from the tragedies of the Holocaust.

You have brilliantly captured this next slice of your family's history as they faced many challenges and a harrowing escape.

Judy, I am so proud of your determination and creativity in delivering this wonderful piece of writing .

"If you think there is no way out, remember never ever give up. The darker the night the brighter the dawn"

Gerda Weissmann Klein
Award winning, Best Selling Author and
Noted Speaker
Presidential Medal of Freedom Recipient

Choices

The True Story of One Family's
Daring Escape to Freedom

J.E. Laufer

First Edition

Publisher's Cataloging-In-Publication Data

(Prepared by The Donohue Group, Inc.)

Names: Laufer, Judy Egett.

Title: Choices : the true story of one family's daring escape to freedom / J.E. Laufer.

First edition. | Phoenix, Arizona : Little Egg Publishing Company, [2017] |

    Interest age level: 13 and up.
    ISBN 978-1-881669-06-7 (paperback) |
    ISBN 978-1-881669-04-3 (ebook)

Subjects: LCSH: Laufer, Judy Egett--Family--Fiction. | Hungary--History--Revolution, 1956--Fiction. | Families--Hungary--History--20th century--Fiction. | Escapes--Hungary--History--20th century--Fiction. | Communism--Hungary--History--20th century--Fiction. | Hungary--Social conditions--20th century--Fiction. | LCGFT: Historical fiction.

Classification: LCC PS3612.A94 C46 2017 (print) | LCC PS3612.A94 (ebook) | DDC 813/.6 [Fic]--dc23

Cover, page layout and map: Damonza
Editing: Linda L., Laura S., Jessica Barranco
Additional consulting and proofing: Nathan Laufer,M.D.
Author Photo: Kelley Kruke Photography
Produced by: Little Egg Pub Co.
Printed in the U.SA

This book belongs to all of you...

To my dear departed dad, whose determination and positive attitude lives on every page. His spirit continues to shine within us.

To my wonderful, intelligent and courageous mother, who shaped our story.

To my loving husband Nathan, and son Andrew who supported and encouraged me to write this book.

To my older sibling, George, who made this journey with me, then and now.

To Annemarie (Just) Strasser and her parents for the overwhelming kindness and compassion they displayed at a very difficult time in our family's history. It was so amazing to finally meet them, so many years later.

To Gerda Weissmann Klein for her wisdom and guidance at various points in my writing.

To all my family and friends, who continued to ask questions, offered suggestions, and pushed me to continue this project.

TABLE OF CONTENTS

Introduction xi

Chapter One: How It Began 1

Chapter Two: Left Behind 7

Chapter Three: Need To Leave 21

Chapter Four: The Train 27

Chapter Five: A Long Trek 33

Chapter Six: The Guards 39

Chapter Seven: What Now? 46

Chapter Eight: The Crossing 53

Chapter Nine: If We Get There 56

Chapter Ten: On The Other Side 63

Chapter Eleven: What Have We Done? 68

Chapter Twelve: The Power of One 74

Chapter Thirteen: Just A Family 79

Chapter Fourteen: No Longer Strangers 84

Chapter Fifteen: Time to Leave Again 90

Epilogue 95

INTRODUCTION

THIS BOOK IS based on the actual personal accounts of my family's escape from Budapest, Hungary after the Hungarian Revolution of 1956. It's a tale of bravery, selflessness, and a little bit of luck. Or perhaps it was divine intervention. You decide.

At the time, I was almost two, so as you can guess, I have no real memory of the events that took place. It was through extensive research that I was able to piece together the story I'm about to share with you.

My father, who is no longer alive, left me a few audiotapes, which were wonderfully detailed. In addition, I've been fortunate to have access to the vast historical archives available through the Internet. And as luck would have it, I was able to reconnect with Annemarie Just, who played an important role in our story. She shared with me her recollections of the events that transpired.

The biggest inspiration and resource for this story, the person who gave me so many of the detailed accounts needed for this book, is my dear eighty-nine-year-old mother, Kati, who is thankfully alive and well.

If I were to sum it up, my parents' story is one of

choices. Some decisions are obvious and easy, while others are much more difficult. And, as I learned while conducting my research, some options are quite dangerous. There are times in life when we may feel we have no choice, but believe me, there is always a choice. It may not be the best or most desirable, but it's there.

This story is a good example of how the choices we make can dramatically change our lives, for good or bad. Everything that occurred only happened because of the brave choices made by various people along the way.

It was my choice to share my family's story with you. And it is your choice to read it.

Our family's story of courage and perseverance has inspired me, and I hope it will do the same for you and generations to come.

J.E. Laufer

DENMARK

RUSSIA

WEST
BERLIN

EAST
GERMANY

POLAND

WEST

HERLANDS

GERMANY

XEMBOURG

CZECHOSLOVAKIA

•Vienna

LIECHTENSTEIN

AUSTRIA

WITZERLAND

HUNGARY

•Budapest

I

MONACO

SAN
MARINO

YUGOSLAVIA

T

A

L

Countries controlled
by Communist Russia 1945-91

"In October 1956, the people of Hungary stood up against the oppression of Soviet rule. The subsequent uprising almost succeeded but the Soviet Union, in a full show of force, re-established its control and the revolution was quashed as quickly as it had erupted…

"Over 200,000 Hungarians fled across the border into Austria and the West until that escape route was sealed off. Thousands were executed or imprisoned"

(Colley, "The Hungarian Revolution of 1956 - a summary - History in an Hour", 2013)

Colley, Rupert. "The Hungarian Revolution of 1956 - a Summary - History in an Hour." History in an Hour. N.p., 21 Feb. 2013. Web. 06 Dec. 2016. Statements about the Hungarian Revolution of 1956

And our story begins…

CHAPTER ONE

HOW IT BEGAN

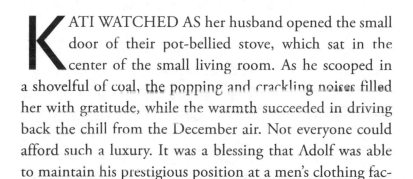

KATI WATCHED AS her husband opened the small door of their pot-bellied stove, which sat in the center of the small living room. As he scooped in a shovelful of coal, the popping and crackling noises filled her with gratitude, while the warmth succeeded in driving back the chill from the December air. Not everyone could afford such a luxury. It was a blessing that Adolf was able to maintain his prestigious position at a men's clothing factory. Such jobs were rare.

She glanced nervously at the far wall. They shared their small two-bedroom apartment with two other families. One of the families lived on the other side of the paper-thin wall, sorely in need of another coat of paint. Usually by now everyone would be settled for the night, but one never knew and she didn't want to risk that their conversation would be overheard. Not when what she had to say was tantamount to treason, a crime punishable by a long prison sentence.

"What's on your mind, my lovely," Adolf whispered

with an easy smile. "You look like you carry the weight of the world on your shoulders."

She looked up into his handsome face, trying to return the smile, but failed miserably. "Tonight, when you went out to get a loaf of bread..." she began, yet her voice wavered.

"Yes?" he said encouragingly when she didn't immediately continue.

"I heard gunshots," came her faltering whisper.

He grimaced. "I heard them, too. It was a few blocks away."

"I couldn't breathe until you returned." Tears loomed in Kati's eyes as she tried to form her words. "Because I feared you wouldn't."

Adolf wrapped his arms around her in a comforting cocoon. "I'm so sorry you were worried."

She cushioned herself against his chest and allowed herself to relax for a moment. He always smelled so good, like lemon and spice.

After a few moments, Kati pulled away and turned to face him, compelling him with her large brown eyes. She shook her head, as she mouthed the words, "We can't stay." her voice barely audible.

"We've talked about this before," he whispered. "It's too dangerous to even think that way."

"It's too dangerous not to," she countered, glancing over at their two small children sleeping in the corner of the room. "Judit and Gyorgy deserve an opportunity to grow up and live a life of..." Dare she say it?

"Freedom," he finished for her.

"Yes." She looked back at him. "They deserve what we never had. Don't you think?"

"The curfews seem to be here to stay," he admitted with a heavy sigh.

His words gave her the courage to continue. "What if our parents had left when the rumors started twelve years ago?"

He shook his head. "Kati, we've been over this. It's not the same thing."

"Isn't it?" She looked away, resting her eyes on their little ones again, her precious children. "How can you be so sure history isn't repeating itself?"

He cupped her chin and nudged her face back until she looked at him. "This isn't the Holocaust."

"If my parents had left when everything went bad, they'd still be alive today." Fresh tears cascaded down her cheeks, but this time she held his gaze. She had to get her point across to him. "As would Emery, Margaret, Joseph, and baby Alex."

Adolf closed his eyes against the pain he felt radiating from her. She'd lost all four siblings, as well as her parents, at Auschwitz twelve years prior. He, too, had lost his sister, his loving sweet sister Viola, but to lose his entire family? It was unimaginable. Tears suddenly threatened to spill from his eyes as well.

"Let's get some sleep, honey," he said. "It's late. We'll talk about this again tomorrow."

Kati nodded and allowed Adolf to gently guide her by the hand. He pulled her from the couch, which converted into their bed. He placed the green pillows with gold trim on the floor before he grabbed the thin strap and pulled out the mattress.

"Tomorrow's Sunday," she said with a yawn. "Let's visit Eva and Janos for coffee."

"It's always good to see your cousins."

"And the children love them so."

Adolf nuzzled her neck. "Your goulash was delicious tonight."

"We were lucky the butcher had meat. I've missed it the last two weeks," she said. "The shortages are getting worse."

"Yes, but remember, we have so much to be thankful for," he said, giving her hand a squeeze.

Kati smiled up at him then looked at her children again. "Yes, we do."

Kati brushed her daughter's unruly blond hair as she struggled to play with her brother. "Hold still, Judit," Kati chided.

Judit said something in a language neither parent understood. "She wants to leave now," Gyorgy said, attempting to translate.

Kati stifled a laugh. "Yes, I gathered that. Okay, I give up. Her curls just won't be tamed."

Adolf scooped his daughter in his arms and tickled her. "My beautiful little girl with lovely golden curls!"

Judit giggled happily, protesting loudly when he put her down. "More!"

Kati shook her head. "We should go."

They walked across the street and down a block to her cousin's apartment building. It was similar in design to theirs and countless others in that part of Budapest, with three families sharing each small space. In her cousin's case, they lived in one of the bedrooms, having sharing rights to a small kitchen.

Eva and Janos greeted Kati and Adolf warmly, before

hugging the children. "Come on in," Eva said. "It's so good to see you! Would you like some coffee?"

The floor boards creaked as they made their way to a small square table. Eva bade them to sit down, while Janos brought a stool to add to the corner. Kati held Judit on her lap, while Gyorgy sat on the stool.

After serving them coffee, Eva gave Kati a piercing look. "Have you heard about the Balko family?" she asked, as she sliced a square of sponge cake for Kati.

"No," Kati replied. "Are they ill?"

"Not ill. Gone!" Eva scoffed. "Into the night, like a bunch of criminals."

The rose color left Kati's cheeks in a flash. She stared at Eva for a moment then said, "I just saw them two days ago. Are you sure they're really gone?"

"Their apartment has been cleaned out. Toothbrushes and all," Janos confirmed with a shake of his head. "Such stupidity."

Kati glanced at her husband, whose eyes silently implored her not to say anything. The warning was completely unnecessary. She was well aware of the dangers of sharing her desire to follow the Balkos' example. She didn't relish the thought of being ripped from her family to spend the next three years in a Russian prison.

"Yes, such stupidity," Kati managed, doing her best to lace her voice with the expected level of contempt. Her hand trembled as she lifted her fork to her mouth.

"Who would do such a thing?" Eva continued, looking deep into her cup of dark hot coffee. "We live in a wonderful country and want for nothing. The government provides for everything." She shook her head. "Leaving Hungary would mean struggling for all of life's necessities."

For the next few minutes, an awkward silence fell. All that could be heard was the gentle sipping of coffee by the adults and the louder slurps of hot chocolate from the children. No one could think of anything to say.

Eva's words had recently been spoken, nearly verbatim, at the last mandatory propaganda meeting. The message had been clear: *Love this country and its occupation. Nothing else would be tolerated.*

The speakers at the meeting had droned on and on for hours about the evils of Capitalism, explaining in great detail how the majority of American citizens were on the brink of starvation. Kati and Adolf had sat side by side, listening dutifully, because leaving early would have put them on the watch list by the guard at the door. Kati had kept her head bowed so that the disagreement in her eyes wouldn't be seen.

Finally, Eva broke the silence by asking Gyorgy a question about his wooden cars. The room was quickly filled with lively chatter. Kati smiled and relaxed, but sought the earliest opportunity to depart, claiming a mild headache.

"I kept worrying they would read my mind," she said to Adolf as they walked home.

"You did well. They didn't suspect a thing."

"I hope not," she whispered, glancing back to their front door. "For all our sakes."

CHAPTER TWO

LEFT BEHIND

THE NEXT DAY, Adolf left work early and walked quickly back to Eva and Janos's apartment. They'd all had little sleep the previous night, because Judit's blanket had been left behind the previous day. She had woken up several times asking for it. Glancing at the horizon, he picked up his pace. Being that it was winter, the sun set so early, making it much colder.

He arrived at their doorstep slightly out of breath and knocked on their door. When no one answered, Adolf groaned. He couldn't return empty-handed. He knocked again and again, a little louder with each rap.

"You looking for Eva and Janos?" a gruff voice called from behind.

Adolf spun around to find an old man shuffling in his direction. "Yes! Do you know where they are?"

He squinted at Adolf. "I've seen you before. Yesterday, no?"

Adolf nodded. "That's right. Our family was just visiting. Eva is my wife's cousin."

"You have two little ones."

"Yes. Do you live here?"

"I'm Sandor," he said with a nod. "The new janitor."

"Oh, good," Adolf said with a sigh of relief. "My daughter left her favorite blanket and I really need to get it back. But it looks like Eva and Janos aren't home yet. Could you help me?" He indicated the locked door with his hand.

"Sure!" Sandor replied with a smile, as he fumbled with his key ring. "I can let you in."

Adolf frowned. While he was grateful he'd be able to get the blanket, he hoped the janitor of his apartment building wasn't so eager to open his door for anyone who asked. It seemed privacy wasn't what it once was. Still, he was thankful that in this case Sandor was there and willing to help.

It took Sandor a few moments to locate the right key. Once he did, he opened the door a crack and called out for Eva and Janos. When no one answered, he took a tentative step through the door.

As soon as Adolf saw Sandor's back tense up, he peeked around the door. "What is it?"

Sandor turned back to him. "See for yourself," he said, his voice tinged with anger.

Adolf's heart beat quickly. From his vantage point, he couldn't see inside, so he pushed the door farther open. He gasped as his gaze swept over the small room. Objects were strewn over the furniture and floor, as if a small hurricane had blown through the home.

"Have they been robbed?" Adolf whispered.

"Don't be naïve!" Sandor spit out, emphasizing his outrage with a stomp of his foot. "Your cousins have obviously left! They've deserted their country, their homeland."

"No. They wouldn't! Why do you think that?"

Sandor shook his head. "Because they're the third family this month! Makes me sick, sick to my stomach. Don't they know how good we have it here?" The janitor ranted on and on, spouting everything Eva had just voiced the day before.

Then it hit him. Everything Eva had said had been an act! Every last word she'd uttered had been a pretense designed to throw them off. Kati's cousin hadn't trusted them enough with their plans, their plans to leave forever.

The shock of that realization made the room spin out of control. He wished he'd known. Then they all could have spoken openly and honestly. They might have traded notes or they could have possibly left together. But, on second thought, that would have been riskier. After all, traveling by foot across the border, burdened with their two young children, was an added risk for any group.

Adolf saw Judit's small yellow blanket folded neatly on the arm of the couch. He couldn't help but smile. It was as if Eva had placed it there knowing that he'd be back to retrieve it. He picked it up and nodded to Sandor who was gesturing dramatically to the walls of the deserted room, continuing his soliloquy about the benefits of Communism. Not knowing what else to say, Adolf left.

The sun was just kissing the horizon as he walked through his front door. When Judit saw what her father had in his hands, she gave an immediate cry of joy. Adolf bent down on one knee to hand her the prized blanket and accept her grateful hug. He then ruffled her hair gently as he stood up. It didn't matter that the blanket had a few stains nor that the edges were frayed. Judit melted into it, making the journey well worth the effort.

Adolf leaned against the wall and watched Kati. She

was mending one of his shirts while Gyorgy played with two small wooden cars nearby.

Sensing his gaze, she turned to him, tensing when she saw his face. "What's wrong?"

Adolf methodically took his coat off and laid it over a chair before answering. There was no easy way to break the news to her, so he opted for directness. "Eva and Janos are gone."

Kati's mouth dropped open. "What do you mean *gone*?"

"They left."

"That can't be!" she cried softly, so as not to disturb the children or the neighbors. "You must be mistaken. We just saw them yesterday, remember?"

"I know."

"Eva went on and on about how crazy the Balko family was, how disloyal and…" She closed her eyes and shook her head. "I don't believe it. Why wouldn't they tell us?"

"They couldn't," Adolf said under his breath. "It's safer to keep quiet."

"But they could have trusted us! We're family."

He looked his wife in the eye and said, "Would you have trusted them?"

"Of course!"

Adolf smiled. "Really?"

Kati sighed. "Honestly, no. But I wouldn't go on and on about how wonderful our country is and how it was an abomination to even consider leaving."

"They had to lie," he said gently.

Kati felt the sting of tears behind her eyes. "I just feel…"

"Betrayed?"

"Yes."

Adolf nodded. "I know. I feel it, too. But I don't blame them."

Kati shook herself and stood up. "This is a sign. We have to go. Now, before everyone else leaves us behind and security tightens even more. In addition, we'll be watched carefully now that my cousin has fled. It's a well-known fact that family members often follow one another across the border. We don't have time to wait any longer."

"Kati, honey, we've talked about this," Adolf began, shaking his head slowly.

"Please." Kati's voice broke slightly. "I know in my heart that now is the time. If we wait, if we don't go now, we may never get the chance."

"It's too risky, too dangerous."

"We have to do everything we can to find a better place for Judit and Gyorgy."

Adolf looked at his son playing on the tattered rug covering the decaying wooden floor. His eyes flitted across the tattered couch, their small table and the peeling paint on the walls. "Things aren't going to get better, are they?"

Kati gave her husband a soft smile. "No, they aren't."

"I know you're right."

She felt an excitement building within her. He was really thinking about it, considering her plea to leave. "There's no hope for improvement, for anything beyond this. None. Not for me, not for you, not for our cousins and not for our children. It just isn't the Communist way."

"You're right," he said with a resigned sigh.

"Wouldn't it be something to have a chance to live in a free country? No one telling us what we can and can't do. No secret police checking on us all the time."

"Not being afraid to be Jewish."

Kati nodded. "And food! Imagine being able to buy meat whenever we want."

Adolf gave her a lopsided smile. "Or oranges?"

Kati closed her eyes. "It's been months since I've had one. It's hard to remember what they taste like."

"I know."

"Can you see it, living in a place where Gyorgy and Judit could have fresh squeezed orange juice every morning?" Kati asked.

Adolf laughed. "That's hard to imagine."

"I know, but it isn't impossible," she said. "I heard in America, people can live where they want, buy the food they want on any given day. No more waiting for the weekend, hoping that meat *might* be available, yet knowing that it probably won't be."

"I'd love to find a house we could own. An actual home with more than one room," Adolf said, allowing himself to dream a little.

"I'd settle for just being allowed to rent our own apartment. A small place we wouldn't have to share with other families."

Adolf slowly exhaled. "That would be something."

"And freedom. The freedom to make decisions," Kati continued. "Our own decisions. Any decisions. Think of all the opportunities America can offer our children. They'd get the best education. They can grow up to be and do whatever they want."

"But," hesitation crept into Adolf's voice, "if we were caught trying to escape…"

"There is danger all around us here, now, every day,"

Kati replied, looking her husband in the eye. "Soldiers fill our streets, carrying guns everywhere, ready to fire on anyone for any crime. It isn't safe and won't be for a long time. Things aren't going to get better. "

Adolf nodded. "The revolution was squashed before it began."

"I was hoping beyond hope that the rebels would succeed."

Adolf nodded. "It looked good for a while, like the Soviets might actually be pushed out, but that only lasted a week."

"I remember the day when waves of troops descended upon us," Kati said with a shudder. "The sound of marching footsteps hitting the pavement, wiping out any hope for change, for freedom. It was all squashed like a bug on the street beneath their boots."

"I think that was their purpose. To remind us that we really had no chance against the *great Red Army.* It worked, unfortunately. How could we fight against such firepower and strength?"

"Adolf, they will never give us a chance to truly live. If we want a good life for our children, we must leave."

Adolf studied her determined and penetrating look then sighed. "You're right. I know you're right. But what do you propose we do?"

Kati stood up. "Let's just go. Tomorrow."

"Tomorrow?" Adolf cried then quickly surveyed the room to see if the children had heard. Lowering his voice, he said, "How could we leave so soon?"

"I don't think we have a choice. It's how it has to be."

"Things like this require planning, time," he said in a

frantic whisper, running his hand through his hair. "We can't just pick up and leave in a single day."

Kati leaned closer, her voice barely above a whisper. "We can tell people we're visiting family in Kapuvar. It's not even a lie, as I think that's the direction we'll need to go. It's close to the Austrian border, so I'm sure someone will be able to get us across."

Adolf shook his head to try to clear the confusion. "But tomorrow? It's so soon."

"If we're going to do this, it has to be now."

"But what about my mother and my brother?"

Kati caressed his cheek. "Of course we'll tell her. And your brother, Max, too. But no one else."

"Okay," Adolf said, nodding. "I know you're right."

She threw her arms around her husband and squeezed him tightly. "Thank you! Thank you!"

He hugged her back. "It's scary. Leaving everything we know behind. But I'll have what matters most to me in the world—you and the children."

Kati allowed herself to remain in his embrace for a few more moments before she pulled away. "We need to visit your mother right now. I don't want to rush your time with her, as I'm sure she'll have lots of questions. Then we need to get back here and prepare. There's a lot to do to get ready!"

Adolf nodded, looking visibly overwhelmed. "What do we take and what do we leave?"

"Don't worry," she said. "We'll figure it out."

They packed up the children and took a short streetcar ride to his mother Rosa's house. The children, oblivious to the nervous stress of their parents, were thrilled with the unexpected adventure of public transportation. Kati smiled as Judit and Gyorgy soaked in every moment of the experience. The jolt of the sudden stops and people pushing their way in and out, was all part of the ride .

When they arrived, Rosa tentatively opened the door. When she saw them all standing in the hallway outside her apartment, her face broke out into a huge smile. She turned back to Max, who crossed the small living room to join them.

"Look, Max, at how much Gyorgy has grown," she cried as the little boy threw his arms around her ample body. "And how handsome you are!"

Max grinned at his mother. "We just saw them a few days ago."

"A grandmother can dote," she said.

Max walked over to shake Adolf's hand. "How are you?"

"Good, good. And you?"

"Fine. Mother's lungs are still bothering her, but today's been better."

"I'm glad to hear that."

Little Judit waited patiently for her turn and was soon rewarded with a dozen kisses and hugs from her grandmother. She giggled appreciatively and returned the affection with gusto.

"You are so beautiful," Rosa whispered. "Just like your mother and father."

When Rosa had finished hugging the children, Adolf said, "Come, Mama, have a seat. We have something to tell you."

She tensed at the tone of his voice. "What is it?" she asked, glancing quickly at her daughter-in-law.

Kati gave the older woman what she hoped was a

reassuring smile despite her hammering heart. Still, she remained carefully silent. It was best that this news came from her husband, not her.

Once Rosa was seated, Adolf held his mother's hands in his. They felt cold and frail, which gave him pause. Closing his eyes, he said, "There's no easy way to say this, but we've decided to leave Hungary as soon as possible. It just isn't safe here any longer."

Rosa stared at her son in disbelief. Adolf shot a quick glance toward Max, who gave him an understanding nod. Adolf was relieved that his brother was taking the news well.

After the moment of shock wore off, Rosa pulled her hands back to cover her mouth, staring at her son with wide eyes. "No! You can't leave!"

"We must," Adolf said gently. "For the children, we must."

"For the children?" It was more of an accusation than a question. "Why do you think it will be better for them to leave the only country they've ever known? In a new, strange place, surrounded by people foreign to them?"

"It can't be worse than living in a country without freedom." Adolf was careful to keep his voice calm. "It's become too dangerous here with the gunfire in the streets. There's far more opportunity for us across the border."

Adolf looked to his brother with a silent plea for help. They'd always been close and he knew he could count on Max.

Max caught Adolf's look and turned his attention to his mother. "Listen to him, Mama. If I had children, I'd probably leave, too. This just isn't a safe place to raise a family anymore."

Rosa considered his words for a moment then turned to Adolf. "Please think about this, my son. You have such a good job here in Budapest. I know quite a few people who would give anything to have the management position you hold."

"I know. I've been fortunate."

"And you're willing to give that up? If you leave, you'll be a stranger, an immigrant. Who will hire you? Where will you live?"

"We'll find work," Adolf said with a confidence that didn't match his inner fears. He pushed away his thoughts that mirrored the look on his mother's face.

"You don't know that!" Rosa cried. "It will be very hard out there, especially with so many families fleeing every day. Three families from this neighborhood left just this week!"

"We'll manage," he persisted.

"But you'll be just one of many."

"Kati and I feel strongly about this, Mama," he said, putting his hand on Kati's knee. "We've made up our minds."

"But," Rosa tried again. She paused, seeming to search for the right words. "Have you thought about where you will go? What's your plan?"

"Kati has relatives a few hours west of here, in Kapuvar. We'll start there then find someone to help us cross the border into Austria."

"That's not much of a plan," his mother muttered, not looking Adolf in the eye. She wiped her right eye quickly before she continued. "What will happen to my grandchildren? When will I see them again?"

"As soon as we can arrange it," Kati said. "It might take a few years, but we'll find a way to visit."

"Or maybe even have you visit us," Adolf said with a smile. "Wouldn't that be nice? And in the meantime, we'll write as often as we can."

"It's not the same," Rosa said, continuing to wipe her eyes as the tears flooded down her cheeks. "I can't imagine not seeing all of you for so long."

They were all silent for a moment, as Rosa quietly cried. Adolf couldn't think of anything else to say to comfort her. He felt torn. It was the toughest part of this decision—leaving family behind.

After a few minutes, Rosa lifted her head, looking resolved to keep her emotions in check. "You'll need money to feed your family and to find a place to live. How can you expect to survive with just the clothes on your back? You'll be paupers on the street. And any guide will want cash to help you across the border. Lots of it, from what I hear. And some will want to steal your money and turn you in…" The words proved too much for her and her voice broke. Her body began to tremble as she buried her face in her hands again. Fresh tears spilled onto her skirt.

Adolf waited for his mother to accept what was inevitable. He reached out a hand and stroked her back, soothing her with comforting words. When her sobs subsided, he said, "We have some money saved. And Kati has her four gold watches that we'll take with us for insurance. You really don't need to worry about us."

"Did you say four gold watches?" Max interjected. "How did you come by those?"

"It's a long story," Kati said.

"But it sounds like a good one." Max sat on the arm of

the couch and folded his arms over his chest as if settling in to listen.

Kati smiled. "Before the war, my father had collected a bit of money. He feared the worst when the Nazis took over and things became so difficult for us…for all Jews. He converted the cash he had into gold, the four watches, along with some other jewelry. He felt certain gold could survive any economic disaster."

"Smart man!" Max exclaimed.

Kati nodded. "As a child, I knew nothing of this. It was only a few years after I returned to Budapest that my cousin, Peter, visited me one day to tell me that the watches had been discovered during the renovation of my parents' old home. You see, he's a carpenter who'd been hired by the government to fix up our old home, so it could be turned into apartments. When he found the watches in the attic, he immediately reported it to his superiors. Peter has always been an honest man. The watches were then turned over to the police. It was quite a surprise to learn that anything had survived. I'd thought our family had lost everything."

"Incredible," Max said.

"Adolf and I went to Kapuvar and paid the police a small fine to retrieve my family's heirlooms. I'm pretty sure my father had other jewelry hidden as well, but my guess is that some of the workers weren't quite as honest as Peter. But I'm grateful to my cousin that he did all he could to find me."

"It was a miracle," Rosa said in awe.

"You're right. It was," Adolf said with a vigorous nod. "We have a lot to be grateful for."

"And because of this, we'll always have some small measure of security, wherever we go," Kati said.

"In addition, Mama, we've saved some cash over the years," Adolf said with a smile. "So, God willing, we will have the means to not only make this journey, but also to start our new life."

Rosa gave him a resigned look but slowly nodded. She looked over at Judit and Gyorgy, who were playing in the corner of the room. "I'll miss them terribly."

"I know you will," Adolf said. "And they will miss you. As will we. But we must leave."

"I'll stay, Mama. I'll be here to take care of you," Max said. "They really do need to escape this place. Judit and Gyorgy will have a much better chance in this world if they can grow up away from Communism."

"I don't agree," Rosa said with a shake of her head. "They'll be safest here. This is their home."

Adolf stood up and pulled his mother into an embrace. "You'll see. We will make a new home and it will all work out."

Rosa looked up into her son's warm eyes. "Is there *anything* I can say to change your mind?"

He shook his head slowly. "We've made up our minds."

She looked over at Kati, who nodded her head in support of her husband's words. Sighing, Rosa pulled away and said softly, "Please be careful. I love you all!"

"We will, Mama," Adolf said. "Don't worry. Your grandchildren will be safe. I promise! We love you both, too."

CHAPTER THREE

NEED TO LEAVE

B Y THE TIME the sun had peeked out over the horizon the next morning, Kati and Adolf had already built up a sweat. Sorting through a lifetime's worth of possessions was emotionally and physically draining. It was still hard to part with so many keepsakes.

"It's going to help that we can claim we're going on a family visit," Kati said, wiping her brow. "That way we can get away with packing a small overnight bag without drawing too much suspicion."

"Others aren't so fortunate," Adolf said. "And we're lucky that my boss allows me to make up the time. Most places are much stricter and they report everything to the government!"

"I don't think I can fit another layer of clothing on little Judit," Kati said, as she struggled to pull the dark blue dress down over her daughter's body.

"You've done well," Adolf said. "Besides, wearing three dresses will keep her warm!"

She chuckled. "I'm so glad we're not leaving in July."

"The layers will help hide extra clothing too."

She looked around the small room. "We need to tidy up a bit and make it look like we plan to come back."

Adolf nodded. "Did you get a chance to let Agnes know we're leaving?"

"Yes, late last night. She seems to always know everyone's business," Kati muttered. "I made a point of telling *all* our neighbors who were awake that we were visiting my cousin, Peter, for a few days."

Adolf rubbed his eyes. "Last night I dreamt that Sandor stormed into our home the minute we left and immediately saw through our rouse. He called the police, who located us a few kilometers from home on the train."

"That's horrible," Kati said with a shudder. "I had my own nightmares last night, but mine involved rabid dogs."

Adolf looked around the apartment. "It's such a pity to leave all the things we have worked so hard for behind. I wonder what will happen to it all."

"I'm sure Max will carefully clear everything out a few days after we leave," she said. "Then this section of the apartment will be quickly filled with another family."

Once they had finished carefully packing the precious few possessions they would take with them, they ate a large breakfast, using up all the perishable food. Then they gathered up the children and their bags and stepped out into the hallway.

As they closed and locked the door, an elderly lady peeked her head out of her door. "I just wanted to wish you safe travels," she said, looking them over carefully. Her eyes rested on the small travel bag.

"Thank you, Agnes!" Adolf said, giving her a bright

smile. "We appreciate you watching over our place for us while we're gone."

"Where are you going again?"

Kati cleared her throat. "Kapuvar."

"That's right," Agnes said. "And when will you be back?"

"In three days," Adolf said. "Just a short trip."

"It must be nice to be able to take a vacation in the middle of the week," Agnes said, her eyes sweeping over them again.

Kati found herself sweating a bit, despite the cold. "One of our cousins is very ill. That's why we're going now. I'm not sure he'll make it to the weekend."

"Oh, I'm sorry to hear that," Agnes said, looking at bit remorseful. "Well, don't you worry about a thing. I'll watch over your place. Happy to help."

When she closed her door, Kati and Adolf both sighed in relief. "That was quick thinking, honey," muttered Adolf as they descended the stairs to the street. Kati looked back, taking a mental picture of the home they'd lived in for so many years, before stepping onto the pavement.

The train station was only ten blocks away, but the early morning was colder than usual with the sun tucked behind clouds. The family walked as quickly as they could, but Gyorgy dragged his feet, complaining with each step they took. He clearly didn't understand why they had to leave the warm confines of their home and tried to duck his face out of the cold wind.

Adolf swooped the little boy up in his arms for the last few blocks. "We're going on a train ride," he promised his son.

"Really? I love trains!"

"I know you do."

"Will it be warm, Daddy?"

"Yes, I'm sure it will be."

"Are we almost there?"

"Yes," Adolf said, giving him a small squeeze.

True to his word, they were on the train within the hour. Judit sat on her father's lap, as Gyorgy craned his body to see everything he could from his seat.

"How fast will we go, Daddy?"

"I think this train might go as fast as a hundred kilometers per hour."

"Wow, that's fast!" Gyorgy said, his eyes wide open.

"Yes, it is. Modern transportation certainly is a marvel." Adolf gave his son a smile.

Both parents were relieved when the children slipped into silence as they watched the rural countryside roll by. Kati allowed herself to take a moment to enjoy the soothing comfort of being gently rocked by the train. As Judit fell asleep on Adolf's lap, Kati looked around the train.

None of the other passengers returned Kati's gaze, everyone seemingly caught up in their own world. She spotted several Hungarian soldiers and two clean cut men. Too neat to be factory workers, she suspected they might be Soviet militia in plain clothes, ready to arrest anyone suspicious. Her stomach churned uncomfortably as she pushed the thought of prison from her mind.

She shuddered as a depressed silence enveloped the train car. There were no cheery conversations, just occasional whispers that died out quickly. That was the way it usually was, the tension so heavy in the air she nearly choked on it.

Kati was thankful that she didn't recognize anyone. The last thing they needed were a lot of nosey questions about their *trip*. Their encounter with Agnes was nerve-wracking enough.

If questioned, she worried few would accept their cover story. Taking a trip in the middle of the week, even with the excuse of a sick relative, seemed like a luxury, what with so many people starving. Would Agnes report them for such decadence?

Lost in thought, she didn't notice the woman who approached her seat until her familiar face was standing over her. Memories of playing in a grassy field and studying with a younger version of the woman in a little one-room schoolhouse flashed through Kati's mind as she stared up at her. "Anna!" she cried.

A few other passengers looked at them, giving her a frown for the inappropriate outburst of joy. Kati blushed then lowered her voice to a whisper. "How have you been?"

Anna brushed a lock of graying brown hair behind her right ear before bending down to kiss Kati on both her cheeks. "Good. And you?"

"Fine," Kati said, feeling her body tense as her old school friend embraced her. She was torn between wanting to reminisce over their early childhood and wishing Anna would just continue walking. It was so good to see her, but any conversation now was risky.

Anna frowned and sat down on an empty seat across from Kati, studying her carefully. "Where are you heading?"

Kati shifted uncomfortably in her seat under her friend's scrutiny. "Kapuvar. Just taking a short trip to visit an ill relative." She was so nervous she couldn't meet her friend's piercing gaze. She simply couldn't trust herself enough with the lie. Anna knew her too well not to see through her.

Anna nodded. She looked around casually, before leaning forward. Then she mouthed the words, *Are you leaving?*

Kati's breath caught in the back of her throat, nearly gagging her and producing a strangled gasp. Adrenaline shot through her as she glanced at her husband. His lips were formed in a taut frown.

Kati slowly turned back to Anna, knowing that her reaction had just revealed all their secrets. Still, she couldn't bring herself to admit Anna was right. Not out loud.

When Kati only stared at her, Anna simply nodded. "I know someone," she said, her voice drifting quickly on an exhale. She pulled out a piece of paper and jotted down a name and address. "Go to Sopron, not Kapuvar. Good luck."

Kati's mouth dropped open. She handed the note to Adolf, who mouthed *Thank you* to Anna as he stuffed it in his shirt pocket.

Standing up, Anna cleared her throat and gave a small laugh. "It was good to see you again. Have a good trip! It will be good to see you in the spring when I visit Budapest."

"Yes, that will be lovely," Kati replied. "See you in the spring!"

Kati smiled in farewell and watched Anna walk into the next train car. Looking around, she was relieved that no one seemed to have noticed their conversation. As she had hoped, everyone was wrapped up in their own world, their own problems. A somber silence prevailed once again.

CHAPTER FOUR

THE TRAIN

W HEN THE TRAIN stopped in Kapuvar, Kati
and Adolf looked at each other. Kati curbed her
impulse to stand up and drag her family off of
the train. Half the train had emptied onto the station's
platform and it seemed strange for them not to get off as
well. They didn't have much of a plan, but the one component they had resolved—finding a way to cross through
Kati's old hometown—had just abruptly changed.

"I grew up here," Kati said wistfully. She looked out
the window and across the train station to the bustling city
beyond. "I don't know Sopron."

"It's not too late. We could get off," Adolf said. He
glanced at his watch. "The train's ahead of schedule, so we
have another few minutes to decide. We still have a choice."

She shook her head at her husband. "No, let's go to
Sopron. We might have trouble finding someone here.
Honestly, I have no idea where to start looking for a guide."

"Okay. I agree."

"It's a sign, don't you think?" she whispered. "My old

friend showing up with the information we so desperately need. Someone somewhere is looking out for us.

"My thoughts exactly." Adolf smiled at his wife and took her hand in his, squeezing it softly. "A higher power is surely watching over us."

As the train pulled out of the station in Kapuvar, Kati felt her heart leap within her chest. She closed her eyes and vowed to stop second-guessing her decisions. There would be many choices along the way and she would have to resist getting bogged down with doubt and worry, every time.

It wasn't long before the train pulled into the Sopron station. Adolf absently fingered the slip of paper with the name and address on it in his pocket. This was the first step of what might be a long and dangerous journey. "Ready?" he asked.

Kati nodded, not trusting her voice to remain steady. She hated the feeling of fear that crept through her, and pushed it aside like a pile of dirty laundry to be handled another day. Fear wouldn't stop her. Nothing would. She wouldn't let it. Standing up, she took Gyorgy by the hand, as Adolf pulled Judit into his arms.

It wasn't hard to find the contact's home in Sopron, as it was located just off of a main street. After a twenty-minute walk, they knocked on the guide's door. Kati held her breath as the seconds ticked by. What if he wasn't home? What if they had taken their chance on this strange town for nothing?

They stood there in silence, listening and hoping for any sign the guide was home. Finally, a creaking noise sounded on the other side of the door. When the door opened, Kati looked the slender man up and down and relaxed. He was a bit younger than she, but looked her directly in the eye, a sign of confidence.

"Anna Fejes sent us," Adolf murmured.

A flicker of recognition passed over the man's face and he nodded. "Come back after dinner, around seven." He gave the family a small smile before closing his door.

Kati's shoulders sagged as she stared at the closed door. "That's about four hours from now."

Adolf laid a hand on her shoulder and said, "Come on. We'll find something to pass the time."

The sun warmed them as they walked through the large city. The medieval architecture was stunning, with so much history embedded in each building, in every stone. They found their way to a small synagogue built in the fourteenth century. Empty and dusty, it did not seem to be frequented very much anymore. After all, the state did not look favorably upon religion or anyone who still attended services. Walking down a narrow corridor, they discovered what looked like the main assembly room.

"Look at the beautiful craftsmanship of the *Aron Kodesh*," Adolf whispered. The *Aron Kodesh*—the ark that held the Torah scrolls—had an intricate design of grapes and leaves carved into its stone frame.

"It's lovely," Kati breathed, feeling an infusion of calm spreading over her as she absorbed the spirituality of this ancient holy place.

When the children became restless, she realized it would be a good investment to find a little nourishment before their trek later that night. They ventured into a little shop and had tea, while snacking on the remains of the sandwiches they'd packed. The shopkeeper was so enchanted with the children that she gave them each a sugar cookie, earning enthusiastic smiles from both.

As seven o'clock drew near, they made their way back to the guide's home. Upon entering the small apartment, they discovered a dozen or so people milling around. Kati immediately noticed a mother with a young girl who looked to be about Gyorgy's age, leaning against the far wall. Kati gave the woman a tentative smile, which was returned.

"We're waiting for two more families," the guide said. "I usually take ten to twenty people across at a time."

Adolf nodded and found a corner for his family near the single mother. Kati looked over at the raven-haired girl with pig tails and nodded in greeting, but the girl quickly hid her face in her mother's skirts.

"She's shy," the woman said, by way of an apology.

Kati smiled and nodded. "What's her name?"

"Lili. And your children?"

"Gyorgy and Judit. And I'm Kati and this is my husband, Adolf."

"I'm Magda," she replied with a tentative smile.

"You'll need to give them something for the trip, you know," the guide interjected, glancing nervously at the three children.

"What do you suggest?" Kati asked.

He handed them each a tablet. "This will allow them to sleep through the journey. We can't risk any outbursts."

The two mothers looked at each other and silently shared an understanding. It would be impossible to keep a young child quiet without a sedative. Kati grimaced as she realized that they would need to carry their children the entire trip.

Within thirty minutes, the entire group was assembled in the small confines of the apartment. No one spoke above a whisper. Most of them talked about the latest news from Radio Free Europe. Kati was shocked when she overheard that the latest reports estimated over fifty thousand refugees had managed to make it across the border and into Austria. These quiet whisperings filled Kati with hope. If so many others had made it, perhaps they could, too.

Kati looked over at the opposite wall and wondered what the guide's neighbors must think. Surely, if the guide were taking this many people across as often as he claimed, someone was bound to figure out what he was doing. Although, it was obvious that no one had reported him yet. In all likelihood, the guide paid the neighbors to keep quiet. After all, the country seemed to run on bribes. Why would this be different?

The guide went around the room collecting money. He stopped in front of Adolf and said, "I'll need three hundred forints from you."

Adolf nodded as he opened up a secret pocket in his overcoat. As he handed over the money, he asked, "So, how does this work?"

The guide looked around at the five families and motioned for them to gather around him. Barely speaking above a whisper, he said, "We'll need to walk to a particular checkpoint at the border. I've bribed a guard to look the other way so we can cross the bridge."

"How long is the walk?" Magda asked, as she held her slumbering daughter in her arms.

"About twenty kilometers."

Kati exchanged looks with the other mother. Carrying

a toddler twenty kilometers wouldn't be easy, but each mother knew they'd crawl a thousand more if it meant securing freedom and new way of life for their children.

"When do we leave?" Adolf asked.

The guide raised a single eyebrow and said, "Now."

CHAPTER FIVE

A LONG TREK

"**W**E'LL LEAVE THE apartment in small groups and meet at a rendezvous point," the guide said, pulling out a sketched map of the route they would take. The scribbled lines showed the path to a building at the edge of a rural area just outside the city. "Here's where we're going. It's a barn owned by an old farmer. He's sympathetic to us."

"Sympathetic to us or just to the money he makes with each passing group?" mumbled someone on the other side of the room.

The guide said nothing and only held the map out for the assembled people to study. They each took turns, committing the drawing to memory. Adolf looked it over carefully, nodded, then handed it to the next person.

When the last person gave the map back to the guide, he said, "Leave in groups of two or three, five minutes apart. We can't be seen leaving all together."

Everyone in the room nodded. The parents with the sleeping children opted to go first, in case they might need a little more time to get there. Kati and Adolf were the first ones out the door.

Kati was thankful that her husband was so good with directions. Her nervousness made remembering any details of the map impossible, but Adolf was confident he could find his way.

A half-moon and star-filled sky lit their way as they walked slowly and quietly toward the rendezvous point. Kati shifted Judit a few times and wondered how Adolf was fairing with Gyorgy in his arms. It would be a long night and she had no doubt that her muscles would feel like rubber by the time they reached their destination.

When they finally arrived at the barn, they waited for the others to arrive. It didn't take long before they began trickling in, with the guide coming last.

He looked at the group and said, "We can talk freely here. Take a few minutes to rest then we'll head out."

The group settled onto the floor. Magda groaned as she settled her charge on her lap.

Glancing sharply at her, the guide asked, "Are you going to be able to make the twenty-kilometer journey?"

"Of course," Magda said, meeting his penetrating gaze squarely. "Don't worry about me."

"Okay then," he said with a nod before glancing at Kati and Adolf. "And you?"

Kati gave him a brief smile, which Adolf matched. "We'll be fine," they said in unison.

"Very well. I just want to make sure you're up for the long trek," he said with a nod. He then turned to address the entire group. "Listen up. I need to give you some instructions. Firstly, and I can't emphasize this enough, everyone must remain very quiet. That means no talking, no coughing, no noises that could draw attention to us. Keep in mind that there might be militia along the path, looking for people attempting to flee. Let me be clear, they won't hesitate to fire on you." He turned to look at Kati and Adolf again. "Even if you're carrying a child. They will show no mercy. To them, you are all criminals."

He paused, his gaze sweeping over the assembled group. When no one responded or looked surprised, he seemed to relax a little and continued. "We need to walk together, single file. At night, the frozen ground can be treacherous. It's slippery and uneven, so we must walk slowly. Do not become separated from the group. If you do, find your way back and I'll take you across another day. Any questions?"

"Where are we going?" one man asked.

"To the border where we'll cross a bridge."

"What will you do about the guards?"

"As I said before, they've been paid well. Don't worry, I've done this before. They know me. Okay, any other questions?"

Everyone shook their heads.

"Good, then we'll head out in another ten minutes."

Kati looked at Adolf and sighed. She wished they could just go now, before she started to talk herself out of the journey. Visions of machine guns flaring in the dark of night, felling her compatriots one by one like doves from the sky, flitted through her mind. She looked over at a young man leaning against the barn's wall. "You can't be more than sixteen."

The boy tipped his hat. "Seventeen, ma'am."

"What's your name?"

"Gabor."

"I'm Kati," she said. She glanced at his right shoe and frowned. It had a small hole on the top. "Is that a bullet hole?" she asked incredulously.

He lifted his chin a notch. "From the Revolution."

"Were you injured?"

He grinned. "No, just got this keepsake."

"What happened?"

"I was shot at from a sniper on the rooftop. Truth is, I got lucky. It clean missed my toe."

Kati shook her head. "That's amazing!"

They fell silent again, the tension in the air mounting as they waited for the guide to come back and signal them to leave. As they all stood up, Kati tried to mentally ready herself for the journey.

"We'll be fine. We have to be," Adolf said with a gentle smile. "Just focus on our children."

Kati instantly felt reassured. She couldn't do this without him, without his strength and confidence. She turned around and gave Magda a reassuring smile, briefly wondering what she would do if she were in the young mother's place. Going through this alone couldn't be easy.

As they made their way outside, Kati was relieved that the air was still, giving them some relief from the freezing wind. She kept her thoughts on the freedom they would soon have, hoping they would keep her warm.

The small group slowly made their way through icy fields and sparse forests. Kati was grateful they had found a guide, for she was certain that she would have gotten turned around if she were on her own. She had heard too many stories of people trying to escape, only to end up running around in circles to avoid arrest, and never finding the border. Tragically, in this weather, they often froze to death.

Kati walked ahead of her husband, looking back at him from time to time. Her adrenaline kept her from feeling her sore muscles for the first few kilometers, but after two hours of cradling Judit, her arms ached furiously. She focused on the simple task of placing one foot in front of the other, thinking of the bridge far ahead of them. The uneven frozen ground beneath their feet was slippery enough without the addition of those small stones scattered throughout.

Suddenly, she heard a sharp cry of pain from behind her. Spinning around, she found Adolf lying on the ground. He'd managed to keep Gyorgy safe in one arm, but was clutching his right ankle with his free hand.

The guide circled back with a frown. He bent down and whispered, "Is it broken?'

"No," Adolf said. "I just twisted it. I'll be okay."

The guide helped him up and Adolf's face grimaced in pain as he tested his weight on that foot.

"You sure?" the guide asked, his brows furrowing.

"Yes," Adolf said with a tight smile. "I can walk on it."

"Very well then. If you change your mind and feel you can't keep up, just make your way back to the barn and I'll collect you when I return."

Fearing the worst, Kati insisted that Adolf walk ahead of her, so she could keep an eye on him. He limped noticeably, but with each step, she could tell the pain was lessening as his gait became more steady.

The young man, Gabor, offered to help carry Judit and

Lili for a few kilometers each. Kati readily agreed and found the walk much easier without the extra ten kilos to carry. Magda looked equally grateful for the young man's help.

By the time Kati took Judit back, they were close to their destination. Feeling fortunate that there had been no signs of other travelers or militia along the way, Kati felt a new burst of energy course through her. She was sure they were approaching the border, having already walked for six hours or more.

Each crunch of her footsteps on the frozen terrain reminded her that she was getting closer to her destination. She was moving steadily toward freedom for her children, toward a new way of life.

CHAPTER SIX

THE GUARDS

A S THEY TROMPED through barren fields, the soft sound of their marching footfalls lulled Kati into a rhythm. The sun was just beginning to rise when the guide suddenly stopped and held his right fist up. Her heart leapt as the entire group halted in their tracks. They all silently gathered around the guide, waiting for him to speak.

He pointed to the edge of the adjacent wooded area and whispered, "The bridge is about two kilometers up ahead. But the guard station is only a half a kilometer away. Keep calm. Remember, I have this all under control."

Kati looked to her husband. The hesitation in his eyes made her realize how crazy the whole plan seemed. They had put their complete trust and faith in this one man, investing a huge sum of money in someone they had met only hours before. After all, his fee was enough to buy clothes for their family for a full year. Her mind suddenly reeled off a slideshow of images as she imagined what could go wrong.

Adolf looked into her large brown eyes and smiled. "Everything will be fine," he whispered. "We've made it this far."

She nodded and struggled to gulp back her gnawing fear. She held Judit in her arms, giving her daughter a little squeeze. There was no turning back. It wasn't an option, but she couldn't shake the nagging feeling of impending doom as they continued toward the guard station.

As promised, it wasn't long before they could see a small structure, well lit by lanterns. Off to one side was a long building with no windows. Taking the next few steps was one of the hardest things Kati had ever done. She struggled against the urge to bolt back into the nearby woods.

As the bedraggled group made their way forward, one of the guards came out of the hut. His large hulking figure and face that could have been carved from granite for all the warmth it held instantly terrified Kati. He swung his machine gun off his shoulder and around in front of him, pointing it into the center of the group. "Halt!" he barked in Russian.

Two more large and intimidating guards came out of the station behind him. They were all dressed in black and each carried a gun.

Everyone immediately obeyed, but looked over to the guide for some kind of explanation. When he didn't say anything, the tension mounted.

"Where do you think you're going?" the first guard asked.

The guide paled as his mouth dropped open. "Wh... where's Anton and Ivan?" he stammered in Russian.

"They finished their shift early today," he answered, furrowing his brow. "Why?"

"No…no reason," the guide said, looking back at the people he'd brought. His eyes held fear and a trace of an apology. The once overly-confident guide was now frozen in place and seemingly mute. It was suddenly clear that his luck had run out.

Kati closed her eyes and prayed. In mere seconds, their future had gone from looking rosy to being quite grim. She and her family were standing in the middle of a Russian guard post, facing down the barrels of three machine guns.

Considering anyone trying to escape Hungary as criminals, these guards would be well within their rights to fire on them. No one would question their deaths. In fact, this guard might receive a medal for his service to the Motherland, protecting Her from traitors and dissidents. Kati and her family would be dumped in an unmarked grave in the middle of nowhere, mere steps away from freedom.

As Kati feared the worst, the lead guard studied the group, his dark penetrating eyes sweeping over the women and children. His gaze lingered on Judit as he decided their fate.

Finally, he spoke. "You'll all need to come with us."

Kati noticed that he kept his gun trained on the group as he marched them all to the adjacent building. Flashbacks of her family being separated at the Auschwitz train station, marching away from her toward another such building so long ago, almost overwhelmed her. The retreating figures of her parents and siblings had been engraved in her mind, a permanent image of the last time she would ever see them alive.

"You will wait here." The guard's voice penetrated her fog, piercing through the memory and forcing her to return to the present. "If anyone tries to leave, we *will* shoot you."

"What now?" an elderly man whispered when the lead guard left the building. Two guards stood by the entrance, watching them silently.

The guide shook his head. "If we're lucky, they'll send us back to Budapest. We may face some charges and perhaps have to pay some fines."

"*If* we're lucky?" the man choked.

The guide looked him in the eye. "Yes."

"And if we're not?" someone else asked.

The guide broke eye contact and sat down on the ground, rubbing the ache and tension from his thighs. "I'd rather not think about that."

Kati followed his lead and sat down on the ground, feeling instant relief in her legs and arms as she laid Judit in her lap. Adolf sat beside her.

"If the guards were going to shoot us, they would have done so when we arrived," Adolf whispered to her.

She leaned against him. "I hope you're right. I'm so thankful our children are still asleep and didn't see any of this." Kati looked at the two soldiers at the door and wondered how old they were. They couldn't be more than seventeen, maybe eighteen. Their young faces didn't yet have the hardened lines she'd seen on more seasoned soldiers. Instead, they looked over the group with what Kati imagined was a measure of compassion.

After an hour or two had passed, the first guard came

in and ordered them to get up. "We've arranged transport for you. You must leave now."

Kati itched to ask where they'd be going, but didn't want to attract his attention. Fear gnawed at her. Were they being shipped off to a prison or back to Budapest? Or would it be somewhere else? The uncertainty of their fate made her head feel light and she had to lean into Adolf for a moment.

As the group was herded into a canvas-covered army truck, one of the young guards jumped into the driver's seat while the other reluctantly took a spot in the back with them. He looked pale and uneasy as the vehicle pulled away from the station.

The road was filled with potholes, which made the ride very bumpy and slow. Wherever they were headed, the journey promised to be a long one.

Bouncing over another bump, Kati gave the boy guard a sympathetic smile, which he ignored. His eyes continually roamed around the interior, never resting for long on any one point. Sensing his disquiet, the occupants began to chat quietly together, glancing over at the guard from time to time.

"Where are you taking us?" Kati finally asked him.

Startled, the boy didn't answer at first.

"I just want to know," she continued, giving him a soft smile. A sudden hush fell over the other prisoners as they strained to hear his answer.

"Budapest." His voice shook slightly as he glanced over the group. "We're taking you back." Everyone sighed in relief and the soldier's shoulders relaxed a bit. "The government doesn't look favorably on deserters, so please think before you try this again," he whispered.

Kati's eyebrows rose slightly. He must have felt sympathetic toward them to voice such a treasonous statement. It was a tremendous relief to know that they weren't being shipped off to a *gulag*. Russian prison camps were famous for their harsh conditions. Still, she didn't relish making the same arduous trek again, all the way from Budapest. It would be much harder the second time, especially since they'd be watched. No, if they went back to Budapest, they'd probably never escape. The government would make sure of that.

She glanced at her husband, who looked calmer than she felt. Kati leaned in toward the guard and whispered, "Can you drop us at Kapuvar? I think we're on the road that takes us right by there." She kept her voice low enough so only he could hear her. "We have family there and our children need to rest for the night."

"I don't know," the guard said with a shake of his head. "I don't think we can do that. Our orders were to make sure you were all dropped at the main police station in Budapest."

Kati smiled at him then looked down at her daughter. Keeping her voice soft and demure, she said, "This is little Judit. She's almost two."

The guard's expression softened as he looked at her daughter's angelic face. "She's cute."

"Thank you. She'll be waking up soon, waking from a long sleep," she said with an exaggerated sigh. "I'm afraid she won't be very happy."

A brief flash of doubt crossed the young boy's face. As

if on cue, Judit started to stir in Kati's arms, her eyes flickering open. Kati pounced on the opportunity and leaned in further.

"I won't be able to keep her quiet," she whispered, apologetically. "And cranky toddlers can be quite loud."

The boy nodded. "I have three sisters, all younger." His face wrinkled in a pained expression. "I know."

"Then you'll let us stay the night in Kapuvar?" she said, pleading. "For the children's sake?"

The guard grimaced and closed his eyes. She could tell he was torn, so she opted to stay quiet and prayed he'd allow them to go to her old hometown.

After a few moments, he said, "Just one night, that's all. Just so the children can rest. Then you'll need to go back to Budapest the very next day. Okay? The police will be checking on you."

Kati nodded vigorously. "Yes, of course. Only one night. Thank you! Thank you!"

The guard called up to the driver, instructing him to stop at Kapuvar's police station. Kati held her breath, hoping the driver wouldn't refuse or question the decision. When he didn't, Adolf gave her shoulder a small squeeze. She didn't dare look up at him, for fear it would jinx the moment. Instead, she smiled softly and kept her eyes carefully downward.

CHAPTER SEVEN

WHAT NOW?

WHEN THE TRUCK stopped in front of the Kapuvar police station, Kati recognized the building immediately. It was the same one she'd visited eight years prior when her cousin, Peter, had uncovered her father's watches. As they walked toward the entrance, she remembered the fine she'd been forced to pay to retrieve her family heirlooms. It had never seemed right, but one never questioned anything an official ordered. Citizens always had to accept whatever the government decreed, or suffer the consequences.

While the border guard explained the situation to the Kapuvar police officers, the two tall muscular men both frowned severely at the family. Kati and Adolf did their best to look contrite as the two unfriendly officers exchanged words. Finally, when the border guard walked out the door, Kati exhaled in relief. She relaxed further when the loud rumbling of the truck's motor faded in the distance.

The police officers gave them some papers to sign along with a strict warning to be on the train the next day.

"We've already notified the authorities in Budapest," the taller one said, "and they will be checking on you at your home in the next few days."

"We understand," Adolf replied with a nod.

Kati felt relieved, for herself and her family, but was immediately struck with sadness for the others still on the truck. She hoped Magda and Lili would be okay and that they would have the courage, strength and money to try again. She had no doubt Gabor certainly would. After all, he was a resistance fighter, brave and resilient.

"Where will you stay while in Kapuvar?" the officer asked, his voice clipped. As the man looked at his watch, she could have sworn she heard his stomach growl.

"The Goldsmits," Adolf replied confidently. "Peter and Marta."

It was nearly dark and had already been a full day since they had arrived at the guide's apartment. Kati prayed they'd get released soon. She didn't relish walking through the streets in the middle of the night, or knocking on her cousin's door after they'd gone to bed. With any luck, this officer was ready to head home for the night and would expedite their release.

"And tomorrow, you'll leave for Budapest?"

"Yes, we promise," Adolf said.

The man nodded. "Fine. Just make sure you're on the train. You have twenty-four hours."

Adolf and Kati nodded and smiled at the man. "Thank you, sir," Adolf added.

"This will be your last warning!" the officer barked as he ushered them all out the door.

Not wanting to take any chances the officer might

change his mind, Kati and Adolf walked as fast as they could away from the station. When they turned the corner, they leaned against a brick wall for a moment, their bodies slumping slightly.

After a few moments, Adolf asked, "Do you remember where your cousins live?"

"Close to my old childhood home," she answered. "About twelve blocks from here. At least, they did eight years ago when I last came back here. I hope Peter is still here."

"Don't worry, dear," he said. "It will all work out. You'll see. We're alive and that's all that matters."

Despite her fears, Kati didn't contradict her husband. Yet, she did silently question his assessment of their situation. How could she not worry? Even after traveling for two whole days, they had not made it out of Communist Hungary. They were no closer to freedom than before. She was tired and all of her muscles ached. A small part of her wanted to give up and just return home, but she knew things would only get worse.

As if he could read her mind, Adolf leaned in and said, "Despite everything, we weren't harmed and we weren't put into prison. And as long as we're alive, there is always hope."

Kati looked up at her husband and smiled. "I've always loved how you look at the world."

He gave her shoulders an affectionate squeeze. "We have a lot to be thankful for."

It didn't take long for them to find the Goldsmits' house. They knocked on the door and Kati was relieved when Peter opened it immediately, greeting them with a broad smile and warm embrace.

"What a wonderful surprise!" he said. "Come, Marta. Look who has come to visit!"

As they walked into the small home, a jovial woman with long graying hair embraced them all enthusiastically. As Kati was pulling away from Marta, another woman Kati's age, her cousin's daughter, emerged from the kitchen area.

When she saw Kati, she cried out with joy. "Kati! Is that you?"

"Yes, Elizabeth," Kati said, falling into her arms. "How long has it been?"

"Ages," the other woman breathed. "Come. You must be hungry. Let's feed you and we can catch up. We were just about to sit down for dinner."

Kati shook her head. "Please don't go to any trouble on our account."

"We can stretch the soup," Elizabeth said with a smile.

Kati allowed herself to be led to a small dining table in the corner of the large living room. They all crowded around it and shared the thin vegetable stew. After being awake for so many hours and barely eating anything, the soup tasted truly delicious.

As Elizabeth ladled a second helping for Kati, she asked, "Are you still thinking of crossing the border?"

Kati's heart stopped beating for a moment and her hands hesitated in mid-air as she reached for her bowl. She looked to Adolf who nodded slightly. "Maybe," Kati said. Accepting the bowl, she continued. "Yes. We tried at Sopron and failed."

Peter nodded. "I'm so sorry. Are you all okay?"

"Yes, but it was a rough night," Kati said.

"What will you do now?" he asked.

Kati looked to Adolf again, who sighed and said, "We're not sure."

Kati pulled his hand into hers. "We should try again. If we go back to Budapest it will be ten times harder to leave again. We'll never have the courage."

"I know."

"We should try from here," Kati said. "It will be easier, because we're closer to the border. That was the original plan before we met Anna."

Adolf grimaced. "I don't know."

"We can't go back to Budapest," she whispered to him.

"Let's discuss it in the morning, after we've had a good night's rest."

Kati nodded as she sipped on the hot liquid, then gave her cousins a brief overview of the last day and a half. The adrenaline had kept her going through the ordeal, but now that she was fed, safe, and warm, her eyelids drooped uncontrollably.

Elizabeth seemed to notice her exhaustion and stood up. "I'll prepare a place for you to sleep tonight. There's plenty of space over there in the far corner. And the bathroom's the second door on the left down the corridor."

Kati was grateful that sleep was in her immediate future. She quickly finished the soup and pulled her daughter to a standing position. She removed the extra garments and allowed Judit to sleep warm and comfortably in a loose long-sleeved red flannel dress. Adolf helped prepare their son for the night and soon they were all fast asleep.

It wasn't until mid-morning that Kati and Adolf awoke, feeling refreshed. They had buttered bread and coffee for breakfast, grateful for the hospitality.

As Elizabeth poured them a second cup of coffee, she said, "I think I can help you. That is, if you're sure you want to try again."

Kati looked at Adolf, her eyes pleading with him. "We need to take advantage of this second chance we've been given."

Adolf sighed. "I don't know. If we're caught again, there's no telling what they'll do to us."

Kati held her husband's gaze. "If we don't try again now, we'll never get another chance. It will be too difficult."

"It's just so risky."

"Of course it is. You're right. But we need to try, for the sake of the children. Let's at least find out what Elizabeth has in mind," she said, covering his hands with hers. "Then we can decide."

Adolf nodded and turned to Elizabeth. "Please, tell us what you have in mind."

Elizabeth nodded. "I know someone who routinely takes people across the Bridge of Andau, over the Einser Canal. It seems to be less watched. Plus, it has the added benefit of being an easier trip, because it involves less walking."

"Wasn't the Bridge of Andau blown up two weeks ago?" Adolf asked. "I remember hearing that. Is it still intact?"

"Yes, it was damaged, but people are still able to cross."

"Do you know the guide's route?"

Elizabeth nodded again. "A freight train takes people almost the entire way, bypassing any checkpoint. The guide bribes the train engineer to stop at the edge of the woods for a few moments. That way people can hop off."

Adolf pondered that for a moment then asked, "How long is the walk to the bridge?"

"Less than an hour."

"That's not bad. How many people have made it?" Adolf paused a moment before adding, "And how many haven't?"

"Honestly, I don't know and it is risky, I won't lie," Elizabeth said. "But I do know that he's set to take a group across tonight. I inquired early this morning, on your behalf, in case you wanted the option. The good news is that he said he'd be willing to take your family."

Kati looked up at her. "Thank you so much, Elizabeth! Really? Tonight?" She turned to Adolf and whispered, "What do you say?"

"I don't know," he whispered back. "It's dangerous."

"Yes," she answered. "It is."

"Are you sure this is what you want?"

She thought for a moment and looked at her children still playing in the corner of the room, unaware of what they had been through the previous day or what she had in mind for them that night. The dream of freedom for them, for their children and their children's children was within their grasp. How could she give up on it?

"Yes, my husband," she said, turning back to look him in the eye. "I am sure."

Adolf held her gaze with his for a moment before nodding to Elizabeth. "We would be grateful for your help."

CHAPTER EIGHT
THE CROSSING

KATI'S FINGERS TREMBLED as she buttoned her daughter into the same navy blue jersey dress she'd worn the day before. She did her best to spot clean it so it would look presentable. When she was done, Elizabeth handed her two more sleeping tablets to give the children that night.

They said their goodbyes and gave hugs to Peter and Marta, before following Elizabeth out the door.

She led them through the city, to a home on the outskirts. When she was a few blocks away, she stopped. "You'll be in good hands with Zoltan," Elizabeth said. "I've known him almost as long as I've known you."

Kati embraced her as the sting of tears pricked at the back of her eyes. She wondered if she would ever see her sweet cousin again. Knowing it was unlikely, she squeezed Elizabeth tighter. "Thank you so much for your help. I can't express our gratitude enough."

Elizabeth gave her an extra squeeze before pulling away. "You should go."

"Why not come with us?" Kati said impulsively.

Elizabeth laughed. "Now? Without anything but the clothes on my back?"

Kati blushed. "You're right, that wouldn't make much sense."

"I appreciate the invitation though. Believe me, I have thought about it, but I'm not as brave as you are."

"Does this idea of crossing scare you?"

"No, it isn't that. I'd be willing to put my trust in Zoltan."

"Then what is it?" Kati asked.

Elizabeth paused and just looked at her for a moment. "I don't know what I'd do as a stranger in a foreign land, away from my family and friends. And I'm not sure I'd find work. The fact is that I don't have children to worry about and I don't want to abandon my parents. They're not well and couldn't make the trip."

Kati nodded. It was never an easy decision for anyone. She had many of the same worries. Would someone hire Adolf? Kati wouldn't be able to work for some time as she would have to wait until the children were older.

"It's okay, really. I'm happy to help others who want to leave," Elizabeth said. "I'm proud that I can assist others courageous enough to put everything on the line. Especially when there are children involved. If I had children, I hope I would be strong enough to face the dangers."

Adolf put his hand on Elizabeth's shoulder and said, "We are indebted to you. What you're doing for us and for others is remarkably brave in itself. All I can say is thank you, from the bottom of my heart."

Elizabeth nodded and smiled. "You're welcome." She

hugged them all then she glanced around her and said, "Now, go. It isn't wise to dawdle on the street at night."

Kati nodded and they pulled away. "Thank you again."

Elizabeth smiled, turned and walked quickly, back the way they'd come.

CHAPTER NINE

IF WE GET THERE

K ATI TURNED TO watch her cousin's retreating
back for a few moments, until Adolf gently pulled
her forward. She looked up at her husband and nodded. "It's just that I don't know when I'll see her again."

He gave her hand a brief squeeze. "I know."

"I just found her again and now I have to say good-bye."

Adolf stopped walking and looked at her. "We don't have to
do this," he said gently. "We could wait if you like."

Kati shook her head adamantly. "No, this is our chance. We
need to take it. Now. Waiting would be too dangerous."

"You're sure?"

Kati nodded and started walking. They didn't speak again
until they arrived at the address Elizabeth had given them. Adolf
knocked on the door of the small apartment then pulled Kati's
hand into his as they waited. It wasn't long before a slender man,
who looked to be in his early thirties, opened the door a crack.
He smiled when he saw them and beckoned them to enter.

Once the door closed behind them, he whispered, "I'm

Zoltan. Elizabeth told me to expect you. Her description of you was perfect."

Adolf smiled. "We're grateful for your help."

"It's my pleasure," he said. "I trust that Elizabeth told you that I'll need to collect payment upfront."

"Of course," Adolf said with a nod. "How much"?

"Four hundred and fifty forints."

Kati and Adolf exchanged questioning looks. It was quite a bit more than the last guide charged and would pretty much wipe out everything they had worked so hard to save up. Normally, Adolf would have tried to negotiate a better price, but their options were limited and he recognized that this was not the time to haggle. Adolf raised an eyebrow to Kati as if to ask if she were sure. She nodded immediately.

Watching them both, Zoltan sighed. "You have to understand, there are a lot of risks involved for me. Plus, I need to pay off border guards, the freight train engineer, and various other people in between. I have to give something to the neighbors as well, so they don't say anything."

Adolf nodded. "We know. It's just that it's our last few forints and if this doesn't work out…"

Zoltan smiled. "It will. I haven't been caught yet."

"Yet?" Kati asked, her voice catching in her throat.

"Don't worry. This is a simpler route than the last one you took."

"So, you heard about that," Adolf said.

"Yes, Elizabeth filled me in. I'm sorry that it didn't work out. I think you'll find that this route is a lot easier. It involves much less walking and we bypass various guard stations."

"As long as we make it, it's all worth it," Adolf said handing him a thick stack of bills. "Kati and I are grateful for your help."

Zoltan smiled as he accepted the money. "It's rewarding for me to be able to help so many."

"When do we leave?" Adolf asked.

"Soon. We're waiting for three more people then we'll meet another ten at the train yard."

It wasn't long before their party was complete and they could make their way to the depot, where they'd get on a freight train. The children were already drowsy from the sleeping pills, so Kati and Adolf had to carry them. The easier trek lulled them quickly to sleep. Kati admired her daughter's serene expression as she slumbered in her arms.

When they arrived at the freight train yard, there were nearly twenty people assembled.

"This is my largest group yet," Zoltan murmured. He spent a few more minutes collecting money from the various families then did a head count before leading them to the fifth track. Once he settled the first few into a car, he hiked up to the front to talk to the engineer.

Kati looked up at the train car and shuddered. The last thing she ever thought she'd need to do was climb into another freight car. *This time will be different. Our destination is freedom*, she reminded herself.

Adolf went first, settling his son into a corner of the car, before coming back to help his wife and young daughter. Kati took a deep breath and did her best to ignore the mounting anxiety that threatened to overwhelm her. She settled onto the floor, leaning against the side and waited for Zoltan to return. The wind whistled through the slats of the car, doing little to shelter them from the cold.

Unwanted memories of a different train car filled her mind as she sat there. It was too similar to ignore. Although the memories were from twelve years prior, it seemed like yesterday when she found herself crammed into a cattle car with so many others from her village. Her parents and siblings, along with her neighbors, everyone had been snatched from Kapuvar in the dead of winter back in 1944. Kati was barely seventeen.

Her brother, Alex, had only been nine months old. So young, so fragile, and so frightened. She'd held him in her arms that night, just as she held her daughter now. Judit was a little older and weighed more, but not much. Kati bent down and, with trembling lips, placed a kiss on her daughter's brow. Kati's brother would have been a teenager today, had he not been murdered by the Nazis. At that time, she had no idea that night in the train car would be the last time she'd ever see Alex.

Everyone had been packed in like sardines. No one could sit. As people kept pushing into the car, she and her family were pressed back into others until there was barely enough air to breath. Finally, when at least a hundred people filled the car, it took off into the night toward an unknown destination. No one knew where they were going.

Even today, sitting in this train car, she could remember the overwhelming stench of all those bodies crammed together. There was no bathroom, only a small bucket that served as a latrine that no one wanted to use. Alex had wriggled in her arms incessantly until her mother had taken him from her. Once in his mother's arms, he calmed and fell asleep. It was amazing what children could sleep through.

Even with warning, Kati could never have predicted what the next few days would have held. Nor what kind of hell the next ten and a half months would hold for her and others who were fortunate enough to survive. All she could sense was that something dreadful was about to happen.

When the train car finally stopped and they were pulled off, lively music was playing as if they were part of some festive ceremony. Kati had been directed to the right, while the rest of her family was shoved to the left. A few women led her to a bunk space. Three women were murmuring in Polish near her. Glancing at their gaunt faces, Kati guessed they had been there for some time. One woman with long stringy blond hair broke away from the group to sit across from her. "What's your name?" she asked in broken Hungarian.

Kati sat down gingerly on her bunk. "Kati," she whispered.

"Did you come with your family?" Although her voice was soft, the woman's cold hollow eyes seemed to pierce right through her.

Kati looked around the room, feeling more and more frightened by the minute. "Yes, but they were sent to the other side. I hope to see them soon."

The woman's lips quirked into a slight smile. She pointed out the window and said, "You see that black smoke over there in the distance?"

"Yes."

"That's your family."

Kati stopped breathing. "W…what?"

"Your family is gone," the woman said blandly.

Kati's hands flew to her mouth. "Why would you say such a thing?"

"Because it's the truth."

Kati shook her head. "No, I don't believe you. No one would do that. They…they can't."

The woman shrugged. "I'm sorry, but I'm afraid it's true. You'll see."

The callous woman had been right. That was exactly what

had happened. Kati's innocent little baby brother, along with her entire family, had been executed immediately upon arriving at Auschwitz. Kati would learn later that the cheerful music had been meant to keep the prisoners off their guard and unaware of the horrors that awaited them.

She always wondered why she had been pushed to the right, separated from her family. Why had she been saved? These questions continued to plague her even now, twelve years later, keeping her awake at nights. Perhaps there was something about her youth, something that made her look strong and able to withstand the work required. Perhaps it was simply the luck of her age.

Some days, the Nazis would just demand she move stones from one side of the large yard to the other. Meaningless, endless labor for the sake of labor. Other days, she would need to dig mass graves for the bodies of the less fortunate prisoners who had been executed. Whatever the reason, she'd been spared the gas chamber that first dreadful night, yet the fear that she would be next ate at her.

After three weeks at Auschwitz, Kati found herself on a train to Bremen, Germany, where she'd spend nine months. Food was scarce and the weather was harsh. The day she turned eighteen, she didn't realize it until the evening. Like any other day, she kept her head down and focused on surviving one more day.

Being eighteen, she felt a keener sense of responsibility to create a family, have children and carry on her family line. If she died, the Krausz family would perish forever. The responsibility to ensure her family's legacy lived on fell squarely on her young shoulders.

Finally, three weeks before the war ended, Kati was taken

to Bergen Belsen, another concentration camp located in Northern Germany. Unaware that her ordeal was almost at an end, she endured the harsh march to the new camp. Not everyone survived that trek, but Kati was determined to persevere, no matter the challenge.

The day she was liberated felt more like a dream than reality. Starved, exhausted, and nearly at death's door, she was transported home, given a chance to reclaim her life.

Shaking herself from the memory, she looked around the train car. This train ride was clearly very different. The air was crisp and clean, and although she didn't know what the future held, it held one component—one ingredient she'd never truly experienced before. *Hope*. Hope for her, hope for her husband, hope for everyone who'd escaped before and for those who were escaping tonight. And, most importantly, hope for her children.

She hugged her daughter tightly and vowed to see that Judit lived the life she wanted to live. Freedom to do or be whatever she wanted. Freedom from the tyranny of Communism. Freedom for anyone willing to work hard and without fear of prejudice or anti-Semitism.

It's worth the risk.

"We'll be leaving shortly," Zoltan said, breaking her out of her thoughts. Nodding, she swept the cobwebs of her memories back to the past. As he climbed into the car, he rubbed his arms vigorously. Kati's eyes followed him as he found a space by the wall across from her to sit.

Smiling, she thought, *It will be worth every forint.*

CHAPTER TEN
ON THE OTHER SIDE

O UT OF BREATH, Kati ran through a strange
forest lit by moonlight, crunching over the frozen leaves that carpeted the ground. At least three
Russian guards were chasing them. Or was it four? From the
sounds of the vicious dogs pacing them, the soldiers were
getting closer by the minute. She didn't dare look back or
slow down. If they were caught again, she knew they would
all be imprisoned or shot.

Stopping wasn't an option, but her legs felt like wet noo-
dles as she forced herself to keep ahead of the dogs. They
had to escape. They had to make it across the border into
Austria. She focused on not tripping, while avoiding the
branches that seemed to fly at her with a mind of their own.
Kati clutched her daughter to her chest as best she could. *I
must keep her safe, at all costs.*

Kati's mind reeled as she ran. How much longer could her
lungs hold out at this pace? *No,* she told herself. She couldn't
think that way. She had to continue, had to give it everything she had. If only it were a matter of will power. Then

she could ignore her fatigued muscles and sheer exhaustion, not letting them put an end to her dream of freedom.

"It's only a few more kilometers," came the faint call from Zoltan, who was somewhere ahead of them, just out of sight. "Don't give up!"

A few more kilometers? That wasn't possible! Were they just running in circles?

She felt a burst of adrenaline course through her as she tried to match her husband's pace. He was holding Gyorgy, yet he didn't seem to have any difficulty keeping up. His strides were like a man half his age, his legs leaping gracefully over branches a few meters ahead of her.

One foot in front of the other. That was all she could think about, all she could focus on. Her daughter had quickly become a lead weight in her arms as she struggled for air.

Suddenly, without warning, her foot caught on a branch, but instead of falling to the ground, she descended into a deep pit that seemed to have no end. As she spiraled down further and further, her fear mounted as she anticipated the impact. Just before she hit the bottom, Kati awoke with a start, coated in sweat.

Dawn was breaking over the horizon and she could smell a strong scent of hay. She was safely tucked into a pile of hay by the side of a river. The *other* side of the river. Looking across the Eisner Channel, she squinted as a few scattered images of the previous night surfaced in her memory.

Could it be?

She looked over at her children sleeping under the hay. Her husband had carefully made beds for them all after their long ordeal. Once everyone was settled, only then had he finally allowed himself the luxury of sleep.

Not wanting to rob him of this glorious moment, of seeing the first light of freedom illuminating the sky, she gently shook him awake.

When his eyes popped open, he said with urgency, "Where are we?"

She understood his reluctance to believe they were across the border. It seemed strange to her ears as well when she said, "We're in Austria, my love. We did it!"

He sat up and smiled ear-to-ear. "Incredible!"

It was as if a large weight had been lifted from Kati's chest. Yes, there were obstacles still to face, but the hardest part was over. They were on the other side. They'd achieved their goal of crossing the border and were safe. As she stood up, more and more of the previous night's adventure filled her mind.

Although the train ride had been uneventful, it was frightening nonetheless. Every stray sound from the woods, each odd jerk of the car, the continuous slowing and acceleration of the train had made her tense with anxiety. She breathed a bit easier when they had disembarked a few hours later.

The walk was only thirty minutes and although very cold, it seemed an easy path across roads and fields. When they reached the bridge—the small wooden structure that spanned two countries—Adolf and Kati smiled at each other. They were almost there. Mangled by the explosion that had taken place two weeks prior, the bridge was now narrow but still passable for foot traffic.

Zoltan had gestured that each member of the party should cross one at a time. Kati waited for her turn as patiently as she could. Frequently, she looked behind her, listening for sounds and praying that no one would catch them. They were so close, but still on Hungarian soil. If they were caught, the short distance to Austria would seem like hundreds of kilometers away. Finally, Zoltan signaled that it was their turn. Adolf silently indicated that Kati should go first.

Stepping onto the first wooden plank, she felt a rush of joy and fear as she clutched her daughter tightly to her. Tears brimmed in her eyes with each step she took. The bridge creaked and moved, almost as if it were alive, as if it were urging her on. Would this tortured structure bring them to a new and wondrous place, where they could live a life with a fresh start, full of opportunities? A quiet sense of calm suddenly overtook her as she walked the few dozen steps, bypassing the gaping holes.

Looking over the fragile railing, the Eisner Canal was stagnant below her feet. She was glad they didn't have to trek through the murky water in the freezing December temperatures. As she placed one foot in front of the other, she could sense the excitement of all the people who had come before her along this path. It was as though they had each shed their fear and suppression on the wooden planks below her feet. And she could also anticipate the exhilaration of those who'd undoubtedly follow her tomorrow and on into the future.

Stepping onto the gravel road on the Austrian side of the bridge, which might not have looked any different to the casual observer. Yet, to Kati, the ground couldn't be more different, for this soil now welcomed her and her family. It was a path which would lead them to freedom.

Giant piles of hay dotted the shore of the river, a few steps from the bridge. Smiling, Kati realized they were intended for them, for the successful escapees. How many others had slept within their warm confines on their first night of independence from Communism? She remembered watching Adolf place the hay over their children as she burrowed into the sweet-smelling straw. Almost as soon as her eyes had closed, she drifted into a deep sleep.

"Look, over there," Adolf's voice filtered through her memories, bringing her back to their first morning in a new world. "I think they're coming for us!"

She turned to follow the line of sight his finger indicated. A truck was making its way over to them. Her first instinct was to flee, but Adolf placed a comforting hand on her shoulder.

"I think they're here to help," he whispered.

She took a deep breath and nodded. Looking around, she noticed the rest of the group was rustling awake as the truck continued on its direct path toward them. Within minutes, everyone was standing around the piles of hay, hugging and congratulating each other. Judit and Gyorgy sat up and rubbed their eyes, completely disoriented.

Kati walked over to Judit and pulled her up into her arms. "Don't worry, little one. Everything will be okay. Everything will be better than it has ever been."

Sensing her mother's relaxed mood and the excitement of their companions, Judit smiled and hugged her tightly. When Gyorgy hugged her legs, she bent down to include him in the embrace.

"Where are we?" he asked.

"Home," she responded.

CHAPTER ELEVEN
WHAT HAVE WE DONE?

A S KATI WATCHED the truck slowly rumble toward them on the dirt road, she imagined they probably came daily to check for refugees. It was logical, given that this bridge was the conduit for so many Hungarians seeking freedom from Communist rule.

When the truck came to a stop, a man with a round belly and huge smile jumped out. "Welcome! We're from the Red Cross," he cried out loud in German. "We're here to help you."

He took turns shaking hands with each Hungarian, hugging some, before piling them all into the back of the pickup truck. Kati smiled at the man, instantly trusting him. Not only did he look friendly and helpful, but he appeared to be well fed and happy. So different from the people she was accustomed to seeing.

The trip was bumpy, but they only had to travel a few kilometers. When they arrived, they were welcomed with coffee, hot chocolate, and breakfast pastries. Gyorgy picked up a sugar cookie from the tray and started munching on it, while

Judit selected a small strawberry jam-filled Danish. Kati smiled at how readily her children accepted their new environment.

Looking around, she could tell this was once a local community center. However, now it was a temporary processing terminal for incoming refugees before they were sent on to displaced person camps. She picked up a cheese pastry and took a seat, watching all the people moving around the large hall. People-watching had always interested her, but this was especially fascinating with so many different families to observe. Their excitement, mixed with some anxiety, was tangible.

Kati also enjoyed watching her husband, observing his effortless interactions with others. Kati admired his ease with strangers, an area where she always seemed to struggle, being more shy. Throughout their marriage, she relied on him to introduce her to people.

Adolf walked around the room in a slow circle. He also seemed to be looking at all the people, nodding a greeting to various families as he passed them, smiling to them and accepting their return smiles.

When Adolf nearly stopped mid-stride, she sat up attentively. She followed his line of sight to an elderly man who was talking on the phone. Adolf's focus was fully on this man, who was dressed in black, complete with a hat. He sported a long beard, speckled with white and curly side burns. He was clearly of their faith and looked very attentive to his conversation on the phone.

As soon as the elderly man hung up the phone, Adolf walked over to him. She quickly realized she should be by her husband's side, so Kati picked up a second pastry and joined them, while keeping an eye on her two children. She could only learn so much watching from the sidelines.

Adolf smiled warmly as she approached. "Allow me to introduce my wife, Katalin. Kati, this is Mr. Farber. He crossed over yesterday morning."

"It's very good to meet you," she said, extending her hand to him.

"And you," he replied with a nod. "Katalin's a beautiful name. It means pure of heart, if memory serves."

"Yes, you're correct," she said with a wide smile. "I do my best to live up to my parents' expectations. God, rest their souls."

Mr. Farber nodded in understanding. "I'm sure you do."

Adolf's eyes sparkled. "Mr. Farber was telling me that there will be a Shabbat dinner in Vienna tonight."

"Oh, really?" Kati said.

"Yes, a van will pick him and his family up later this afternoon. I asked if we might join him and he kindly said he thought we could."

"How wonderful!"

Mr. Farber nodded. "Yes, the Jewish Agency is hosting a Shabbat dinner at the Rothschild Center in Vienna. They'll send a van in a few hours. I can't promise there will be room, as I have a wife and three young children, but if there is, you're welcome to join us."

"I hadn't thought such a thing would be possible," Kati said. "Thank you so much!"

"It is my pleasure." Mr. Farber gave her a slight bow and walked over to a small group of men and women, sitting on the other side of the room.

Adolf waited for him to move out of earshot then pulled his wife over to a corner. "If we can get to Vienna, I think we can find an alternative to the DP camps. It's such a huge city."

Kati nodded. Although she understood why Austria had needed to set up Displaced Persons (DP) camps, she couldn't stomach the idea of voluntarily going into one. Although she knew it would be different from the Nazi camps, she still shuddered. There had to be another option.

"Don't worry," he said, embracing her. "I completely understand and promise you'll never have to step foot in another camp of any sort ever again."

She nodded. Prior to this moment, her entire focus had revolved around escaping from Hungary. Now that she had arrived in Austria, she had to shift gears and put her attention on finding a place to stay. So many Hungarians were in a similar situation, homeless without much to call their own. As Austria continued to bulge with refugees, she realized it wouldn't be easy to find a place.

Yet, her shoulders relaxed. She trusted her husband. He'd find a solution. Although he had never looked like he was eighteen years older than she, he had experience and wisdom that accompanied age. Even now, he had found a way to get them into Vienna. He was right. The capitol city would afford more options for them. She smiled up at him, feeling grateful to be married to such a resourceful and loving man.

When the time came, a van arrived at the community center to pick up a dozen men and women for the dinner. It was crowded, but Kati was grateful there was room for her family. The eight-kilometer trip went by quickly as the van buzzed with excited chatter, the occupants sharing the common experience unique to their culture.

When they arrived at the dinner, Kati's heart swelled to see the hall bursting with people. Jewish people—her people—openly celebrating their faith. It was lovely to be in a country where they were free to do so.

When she had returned from the Holocaust, Kati had been so relieved to be free of German rule. However, as the months rolled by, she soon realized that the Hungarian Workers Party was anti-Semitic, too. Jews had quickly learned to hide their religion and blend into society. They feared losing their jobs or enduring public humiliation.

Just after they settled into their seats, three young women lit candles. They ceremonially covered their eyes then a rabbi blessed the wine and challah bread before the meal was served.

Although the Shabbat dinner was a simple meal, it felt like a feast for Kati, Adolf, and the children. The meat was slow roasted and there were plenty of fresh vegetables and loaves of challahs to share.

As the dinner came to a close, Kati felt a new sort of anxiety overtake her. She took each child by the hand and slowly shuffled behind the others toward the exit, delaying the inevitable as long as possible. It would be cold outside and they had nowhere to go for the night. Listening to the conversations of the families around her, she realized that almost everyone else seemed to have family in Vienna. Although it seemed the homes were cramped, those people would at least sleep with a roof over their heads.

A few of their dinner companions had found hotel rooms for the night, but they explained how hard it had been. Most of them had been in Vienna for several weeks, if not months. Kati became more and more depressed as she realized how difficult it would be to find a room. Besides, even if they could find a place, they had so little cash and forints were a currency nearly useless in Austria.

What are we going to do? Where will we sleep?

As the cold winter air greeted them at the Rothschild Center's entrance, Adolf and Kati stopped and looked at one another. Tears pooled in Kati's brown eyes, and they felt like they might freeze. "I'm sorry, darling. I made a horrible mistake," she whispered, feeling the cruel grip of fear creep up her throat.

"What do you mean?" he asked.

She closed her eyes then opened them again, giving him a penetrating look. "We have nowhere to go. No place to spend the night, and it's so cold. We should go back. At least at the DP camp we'd have a warm place to sleep. Otherwise…what will become of us, of the children?"

Adolf returned her look with a soft smile. "You're exhausted, my darling. So am I, but don't give up. I'll figure it out."

"I'm not sure it's possible."

"There's no such word as *impossible*. I will find a place for us to stay, one way or another. I promise you that!"

She nodded up at him, needing, wanting to believe him. He gave her a kiss, which succeeded in casting a momentary warm glow throughout her body. Then he pulled away and left her standing there, leaning against the wall of the building, shielding her children against the cold within her embrace.

Her eyes were transfixed on her husband as he continued down the street. As she watched, he stopped to talk to two women on the corner. When one pointed down the road further, he nodded his head. Then he briefly looked back to give Kati a smile and a wave before he continued down the street. She knew he had no plan, Kati tried her best to fight back her tears and appear hopeful.

CHAPTER TWELVE

THE POWER OF ONE

A S ADOLF'S FIGURE retreated into the night, Kati felt a familiar burst of love for him. He'd always come through for her in the past, but this was different. He'd need to pull off a miracle in this strange city.

As soon as he disappeared around a corner, she walked a few paces to a bench and settled the children against her. She gave them a brief smile as they snuggled contently into her warmth. Rosa's words of doubt flooded her mind. *If you leave, you'll be a stranger, an immigrant. Who will hire you? Where will you live?* Maybe she'd been right after all.

Kati closed her eyes and allowed her mind to drift back in time, to the moment when she'd stepped off the train in Budapest after having been liberated from the concentration camps. She had two uncles she knew who had survived the Holocaust and lived just outside the bustling city.

Although deep down she'd known that her parents and siblings had been killed, she preserved the hopeful dream that somehow they'd survived. Somehow, some way. For years, she cherished that fantasy until she finally allowed it to be extinguished by reality.

When her two uncles invited Kati to live with them, she gratefully accepted. Shattered and lonely, she focused on rebuilding her life. Kati quickly developed a knack for cooking delicious meals despite the food rationing that took place after the war. Her uncles were always pleased by her dishes.

However, it wasn't long before both her uncles were married and Kati was sent to the Hannah Szenes school for girls in Budapest. There, Kati made good friends. Many of the girls had lived through what she had and therefore understood how she felt.

Despite her newfound friendships, happiness seemed a thing of the past, an emotion from a different time. Without family and limited prospects for the future, she'd become lost in a swirl of depression. It was difficult not to continually think what her life was like prior to the war.

Before the war, she'd attended school, had many friends and helped her parents run their general store in the afternoons and on weekends. They'd wanted for nothing. Love and laughter flowed through the community freely. Looking back, it had been so idyllic.

Upon returning to Budapest after the war, everything had changed. It seemed wrong to feel anything but misery. There were few reasons to smile, let alone laugh. And her future seemed destined for emptiness, without anyone to share life's experiences. Gone was any promise of the seemingly normal life she had once lived before the war.

Kati hadn't been expecting her life to change when she

walked into a little shop in Budapest. The fresh smell of spices and baked goods welcomed her as she looked around.

A gray-haired, stout shopkeeper had greeted her warmly, the woman's eyes holding a tinge of a familiar sadness. She immediately handed Kati a picture of a beautiful young girl. "Do you recognize this girl? She would be about your age now. Do you know what happened to her? Were you in Auschwitz? Maybe you recognize her? Her name was Viola."

As if it were yesterday, Kati felt the waves of guilt—the guilt of surviving when others hadn't—hit her again as she dutifully studied the photograph. She dreaded the disappointment that her next words would bring. It was practically a daily occurrence she had learned to endure. Total strangers begged her to view pictures of their lost loved ones with the faint hope that they might have survived the atrocities of the war.

As she held the precious photograph in her hands, the image floated before her eyes. She'd survived when this extraordinarily beautiful girl had perished. She often wished she could exchange her life for the people in the photographs. She'd give anything to bring them back to life.

Her voice faltered as she looked up into the woman's grief-stricken eyes. "No, ma'am. I'm so sorry."

The woman nodded her head, pausing for a moment in what Kati imagined was a reset of emotions. "Come. Have a seat and have some tea. My name is Rosa. Please, let's talk. Tell me your story."

Kati nodded, wiping a tear from her eye. As Rosa poured her tea, Kati poured out her heart to the kind lady.

It had been some time since she'd shared the horrors with anyone and she found herself feeling safe, confiding in this stranger. She really wasn't one to open up easily to strangers, but talking to Rosa made her feel better.

When Kati had finished, Rosa shared her story with Kati, revealing that she had two surviving sons. A warm glow came over Rosa as she spoke of her eldest son, Adolf. They smiled together as she regaled Kati with humorous and touching tales of his life.

As Rosa poured Kati her fourth cup of tea, Adolf walked through the door. Rosa gasped with joy upon seeing him, immediately standing to give him a hug, reminiscent of an embrace for a long lost relative. "I'm so glad you're home, Adolf," she said. "I have someone I want you to meet. My son, this is Katalin Krausz."

Thinking back, Kati remembered being immediately struck by his handsome face and smiling eyes. But that wasn't the most astonishing thing. No, the most astonishing thing was the look he'd given her. Despite the fact that she was a total stranger to him, he'd immediately gazed into her eyes as if she were the only woman in the world.

Kati had been a teenager when she was ripped from her family and dropped into an inhumane place devoid of love, and compassion. Then, later, when she lived with her uncles, she was busy cooking and cleaning rather than socializing. Various young men had given her compliments and admiring looks throughout her early adult life, but she'd never experienced anything close to what she had felt that day with this young man. She'd instantly felt safe in his company.

Adolf and Kati spent the rest of that day together,

sharing stories about their lives. Kati discovered that it was possible for her to laugh and feel happy once more. She even began to feel the seedling of love grow within her, something she had never thought possible. Later, Adolf would confide in her that for him, it had been love at first sight.

Opening her eyes, the smile of reminiscence remained on her lips as she watched a more mature version of her husband walk toward her. Despite the passing years, Adolf didn't appear to have aged. He still didn't have a single gray hair on his head.

As he approached Kati, she carefully moved the slumbering children, so she could stand to greet him. Rising from the bench, she caught his serene smile and threw herself into his arms. She knew instantly that he'd somehow managed the impossible.

CHAPTER THIRTEEN

JUST A FAMILY

A DOLF HELD HER for a moment then whispered, "You won't believe what just happened."

"Tell me!"

He pulled back, shook his head gently and said, "I will, but we need to get going."

He scooped up Gyorgy into his arms, as Kati did the same with Judit. She walked silently by his side following him down the road. She was grateful that the children hadn't stirred.

After a few moments, she asked, "Where are we going?"

"Let me start at the beginning of the story," he said with a smile. "It's a good one."

"Okay, but just tell me if this is going to be a long journey. I'm tired." She cringed at the whine in her voice.

"It's just a couple of blocks up the street," he said. "We'll be there before you know it."

"Okay, good. So, please do tell me what happened," she said, hoping the story would distract her from her exhaustion.

"Well, when I left you, I found two elderly ladies on the street. I approached them and asked if they knew of a place we could stay."

"I saw that," she exclaimed. "I noticed that they directed you down the street."

"That's right," he said with a nod. "They told me to try St. Rochus Church. When I arrived, Sister Grete greeted me. I could tell immediately she wanted to help me. She had such a sympathetic face. I will tell you that I was suddenly grateful for all the German lessons I'd had in school. Without them, things wouldn't have gone as well."

"I wish I'd paid attention better in school," Kati said with a frown. "I might be able to understand a little, but I can't speak German."

"It's no matter," Adolf said with a wave of his hand. "I can speak for both of us and if needed I can always throw in a little Italian."

"I'm not sure how helpful Italian will be, but I admire your talent."

He smiled. "Thank you."

Kati sighed. "We'll need to learn English soon, if we want to go to America."

"We can tackle that when we need to. However, today, German came in handy. Sister Grete immediately went to the phone and called people she knew. I sensed she thought it was an impossible task, but she was eager to try to help us."

"No one can resist you, my husband."

He chuckled. "Oh, I don't know about that. I haven't shaved or showered in days. I'm sure I look ragged. Honestly, I think she was more impressed when I told her about you and the children. Her heart melted at the thought of you tromping through the woods in the middle of the night with two young children. She was moved by your willpower and perseverance."

"Thank you," Kati whispered. "So, she found us a place to stay?"

"No," Adolf replied with a shake of his head.

She frowned and waited for him to continue. When he didn't, she asked, "So then, what happened?"

"Oh, you want to know more?" he asked with a twinkle in his eye.

"Of course I do!"

"Well, that's fine then," he said with a teasing grin that made her heart melt. "As the sister made her sixth or seventh call, a young girl came over to us. I think she'd been curious about all the phone calls the sister was making, so she hung around. When Sister Grete got off the phone the last time, she shook her head sadly, letting me know the family she'd just called couldn't help. It was then that the girl politely interrupted and asked if she might be able to do anything. The girl turned out to be a volunteer at the church daycare. She said she works there almost every day after school and that her name is Annemarie Just. Oh, Kati, she's only sixteen years old, but she is so industrious. And generous. She has offered to give up her bedroom in her house for us!"

Kati's gasped in surprise. "And her parents agreed? That's incredible!"

"Well," Adolf said, looking ahead, "not yet. She said she needed to head home to ask them."

"Hm?" Kati felt a chill of fear creep up her spine.

"It's just that she needs to ask her mother and father first. I went to get you while she did that, so that we'll be ready if it worked out."

Kati's shoulders slumped as she felt the air crush out of her lungs. It was so unlikely that this young girl's parents would agree. After all, how many people would allow four total strangers into their home? Still, she nodded, doing her best not to cry.

"How many children do they have?" she asked.

"Annemarie told me she had two younger brothers."

"Oh. It sounds like they already have a full house," she said, feeling defeated with each step she took toward the church. A sense of anguish threatened to overtake her.

"Oh, my darling. Don't worry," Adolf said, his voice sounding comforting and soft. "It will work out. You just wait and see. I know it will!"

Kati nodded and did her best to believe him. It was hard not to get caught up in his enduring optimism. He truly believed that only good things would come to them. She forced herself to look forward, to hold her head up and capture some of her husband's confidence.

As they approached the tall, wooden, double doors of the church, Kati's mouth dropped open. There stood a man with two children on the front step. *Could it be?*

"You must be the Egetts!" the man said in German, as he reached out his hand to Adolf. "It's a pleasure to help you! I'm Leopold Just."

Kati shook her head, not believing her eyes and ears. "I can't tell you how much this means to us. Your kindness, your generosity. Thank you!"

Adolf translated her words to Leopold, who looked at her with a kind expression.

"Of course," he said. Then, with a laugh, he added, "When it comes to helping others, one should never think."

Kati shook her head in wonder. "We are so grateful!"

"Don't mention it," he said. He gestured to the boy standing next to him. "This is my son, Helmut. And of course, you know Annemarie."

"Annemarie," Kati said, giving the young blond girl a hug. "Words can't express my appreciation to you for your lovely generous heart. We are so indebted to you and your family for this kindness."

As Adolf translated, he smiled at the two women, who were crying and smiling at each other. Although Annemarie didn't speak any Hungarian and Kati's German was very limited, they still seemed to understand each other perfectly.

"Is this baby Judit?" Annemarie whispered, inching toward Kati. "Your husband told me about her. She's adorable. Look at all her blond curls!"

"Thank you. Yes, Judit is nearly two now," Kati said, holding two fingers up.

"We will take you home," Leopold said. "It's not far."

As they walked, Annemarie reached out her arms, asking if she could hold Judit. Kati nodded and watched her daughter slip easily into the young girl's arms, never waking.

CHAPTER FOURTEEN

NO LONGER STRANGERS

WHEN THEY ARRIVED at the house, Kati felt a new burst of energy. Despite her complete exhaustion, she found herself eager to see the home where they would be staying. But more than that, she wanted to meet Anna, Annemarie's mother, hoping and praying that the woman would accept them as eagerly as her husband had.

As soon as they entered the living room, Anna came out of the kitchen with a dishcloth over her arm. She ran her fingers through her short blond hair before coming forward for introductions. Anna's warm, inviting smile told Kati everything she needed to know. They were welcome and safe.

Annemarie then showed them her small room, which was sparsely appointed with a small folding bed, a white dresser, a small table with two chairs, and a few white boxes in the corner.

"Where will you sleep?" Adolf asked.

"With my brothers," she answered cheerfully. "There's plenty of room."

A cocoon of admiration for Annemarie enveloped Kati. This amazing girl had happily volunteered to relinquish her room to total strangers. It was hard to imagine that there were such kind people in the world.

"Would you mind if we bathed the children before bed?" Kati asked in broken German, complementing her words with explanatory hand gestures.

Annemarie nodded. "May I help?"

"Of course," Kati smiled.

Together, they peeled off the layers of dresses from the cranky toddler, who wasn't thrilled to be woken up that way. Annemarie used a sweet cooing tone, which settled her immediately. Judit's frown lessened and she allowed her new friend to continue pulling her clothes off.

"So many clothes," Annemarie whispered. "She must be wearing four dresses!"

"We had to find a way to bring clothes across the border without having too much to carry," Adolf explained in German. "It would be far too suspicious to bring more than one small suitcase."

Annemarie nodded her head, but frowned. "It's hard to imagine all that you've been through. So many challenges."

Adolf smiled. "We haven't been given anything we can't endure. So many other families were far less fortunate. Truly, we've been very lucky." He looked over at Kati. "Very lucky indeed."

Annemarie shoulder's seemed to relax at Adolf's words. She lovingly bathed Judit, cooing words of encouragement at her and making her smile. Kati smiled as she washed Gyorgy, who was reluctant, but not quite as vocal about it. When the children were finally clean, Kati and Annemarie settled them into the trundle bed together where they instantly fell asleep, warm and safe.

When Kati and Adolf tiptoed out of the room and into the living room, they saw Anna and Leopold setting up the convertible couch into a bed. Kati smiled and thanked them. She had been prepared to sleep on the floor, so this was a pleasant surprise. She took a quick sponge bath before getting into bed. It didn't take long before she was fast asleep.

The next two days set a comfortable pattern of activity for the two families. Since it was the weekend, the Justs were home all day. Annemarie found creative ways to play with the children, giving Kati time to rest, catch her breath and become used to her new surroundings. Kati was relieved that Anna allowed her to share her kitchen. Together, the two women made delicious creations for the two families, mixing Hungarian and German cuisines beautifully.

Annemarie spent all her time with Judit, treating her like her baby sister. Kati was amazed at the teenager's ingenuity and imagination. Judit especially loved watching the various puppet shows performed in the theater that Annemarie and her brothers had crafted years prior. Despite the fact that Judit was just learning to speak and didn't know any German, there was no language barrier between them. Even the age gap seemed to make no difference. They allowed their mutual affection for one another to guide their communication.

The two Just brothers took Gyorgy under their wings, sharing their wooden kits and toy cars with him. Kati found herself smiling more and more as she watched them all play as if they'd known each other for years. These kind people had instantly become extended family.

When Monday arrived, Adolf woke up early to visit Jewish Immigrant Aids Services (JIAS), as well as the American and Canadian embassies in an effort to book passage out of Austria. There was a lot of competition for spots on the boats out of Austria, resulting in a long waiting list . Leopold did all he could using his position with the Federal Ministry of the Interior, but the sheer number of people trying to leave was overwhelming.

Fortunately, JIAS was able to subsidize their living expenses, giving them money for food. Kati prayed they wouldn't need to sell any of her father's watches which they'd managed to sneak across the border. After all, they'd need money once they reached their new country.

As Christmas approached, Kati and Adolf found an opening at the Hotel Gabriel only two kilometers away. Although Kati would miss the cozy home they'd grown accustomed to, the last thing they wanted to do was to overburden the Just family, especially as they prepared for their holiday.

The small hotel was quite cheerful with its bright yellow façade. Many other refugees were staying there, each trying to find a way to move to America or Canada, each with a unique story of struggle and triumph. The halls were always bustling with activity.

Adolf continued to seek assistance, pleading for a quick departure date, but after a week of living in the hotel, they realized it wasn't going to be a quick process. They'd need to sell a watch in order to manage their living expenses. Kati sighed, thinking about it. They only had four and that had to last them through to America or Canada. Fortunately, she was accomplished at stretching every schilling.

By mid-January, they received an invitation to celebrate Annemarie's seventeenth birthday, which they happily accepted. Kati had managed to bring a few pieces of jewelry along with them and selected a small onyx ring to give her. It had been a favorite of hers when she was a teen, so she hoped Annemarie would like it as well.

Annemarie was touched by the gift, hugging her profusely. "I will cherish this always!" she promised.

As the weeks rolled by, Adolf had to sell another watch. He was doing everything he could to plead their case with the various organizations and embassies, but there were many families ahead of them. Kati did her best to keep a positive outlook, but couldn't stop the waves of panic from choking her.

"What are we going to do?" she whispered to Adolf one night. The two children were asleep in the bed next to them, so she kept her voice low.

"Don't worry," he responded. "We still have two watches left and have been very blessed so far."

"I know, and I don't mean to sound ungrateful, but I'm frightened. What will we do if we can't leave soon?"

He pulled her into a hug. "I will take care of us, darling. I'll find a way. It will all work out, you'll see!"

"You say that," she said with a frown, "but nothing is happening and the money is running out."

"Something will happen for us soon. We just need to hold on a little longer. Leopold has been so kind to continue to ask around for us," he said with a smile. "Not everyone has someone in the Ministry watching over them."

"We are very blessed to have met Annemarie and her family."

"See? You were worried then, and I told you it would all work out and it did."

"Yes, you did. And yes, it did, but…"

Adolf gave her a lopsided grin. "Please try not to worry until there is something to worry about."

"I know you're right. I just can't help it," Kati said. "I wish I could be like you and be so optimistic."

They both fell silent for a few moments. Then she said, "My two uncles made it to America a few months ago. Perhaps they could sponsor us?"

"I doubt they'd be able to help us much, Kati. Chances are they're struggling to make their way and take care of their own families. The more I think about it, the more I'm convinced that it will be easier to go to Canada. There are too many people flocking to America."

Kati nodded. "Canada would be fine with me. I've heard it's nice there."

"When I was at the Canadian Embassy yesterday, I overheard people talking about what a wonderful country it is. The people seem friendly and welcoming."

"Good," Kati murmured as her eyes began to close. She felt reassured by her husband's words. There was no reason that their good fortune wouldn't continue a bit longer. She prayed for guidance as she drifted off to sleep.

CHAPTER FIFTEEN
TIME TO LEAVE AGAIN

I T WAS A sunny day in mid-March when Anna visited the Egett family with good news. Leopold had managed to secure four seats for them on a plane to Canada that afternoon. Kati couldn't believe her ears. They'd been wait-listed for passage on a boat, but the list was terribly long. They packed up as quickly as possible and headed to the airport.

Kati didn't like to admit it, but she'd been dreading a long boat ride. It would have been an uncomfortable journey, especially with two youngsters in tow. It seemed like a dream come true that they'd be traveling by plane. It was amazing to think that they'd be in a new land of hope and opportunity within a day.

She smiled to herself when she realized that Adolf had been right all along. She had worried about how they were going survive in Austria, about how they were going to leave, and how sick they were going to be on a boat. Yet, it was all needless worry. Everything had worked out just like her husband had said it would.

Kati and Adolf were checked out of the hotel within an

hour and took a taxi to the airport, urging the driver to hurry. As Kati looked out the window, Gyorgy piped up with many questions.

"Where are we going?"

"Canada," she answered. "Remember we looked at some pictures that Daddy brought home from the embassy last week?"

"Yes. The place that has those extra big squirrels with the flat tails and big teeth?"

Kati and Adolf laughed. "That's right. Beavers."

"Will it be cold?"

"I hope not," Kati said, shivering at the thought, "but we'll be happy to settle wherever they'll have us."

"How will we get there?"

"We're taking a plane."

"Really?" His eyes were big and bright. "Will it be a big plane?"

"I don't know," Kati said, glancing at Adolf.

"Yes, it will be very big," Adolf said. "Leopold told me that it was especially made for taking many people far away. A lot of other families will be joining us."

"I can't wait to see it."

"Me, too," Adolf said, giving Gyorgy's mop of brown hair a small pat.

"And I can't wait to see where we land," Kati said, leaning into her husband's arm.

When they boarded the plane, Kati was surprised by how many people were crammed inside. She counted a little over one hundred men, women, and children. Glancing around, she felt a burst of gratitude to all the government agencies which were helping all of them.

The plane ride took nearly twelve hours, but it was uneventful. The children were fascinated by the experience and they even managed to sleep a few hours in their seats. As soon as the plane landed, they went through customs and were directed to a bus.

"Where are we going?" Adolf asked politely.

"The train station, sir," the young attendant said. "They'll give you further instructions there."

The bus ride was short, but Gyorgy had more questions, which Adolf patiently answered. Judit was content to stay in her mother's arms and look out the window. When they arrived at the train station, the official asked if they'd like to live in Winnipeg or Vancouver.

"We can't stay in Montreal?" Adolf asked.

"Do you have relatives here?" the man asked.

"No. No relatives."

"How about a sponsor? Someone who could help you?"

Adolf shook his head. "No, we don't know anyone here."

"Then I'm afraid you can't stay," the official explained. "Montreal is very crowded. We need to send people west. Don't worry. It's lovely, sir. You and your family will love it. And, if after a year, you decide you don't like it we'll pay for your transportation back. You have nothing to lose by trying it, and frankly, there's more opportunity there."

"Thank you, sir. Please one moment." He turned to Kati and whispered, "What do you prefer? Winnipeg or Vancouver?"

Kati leaned in and whispered, "On the plane, I overheard a couple talking about Winnipeg. The woman had said it's so cold that no one ever goes outside in the winter."

Adolf smiled and turned to the attendant. "Vancouver, please."

"Certainly, sir. That will be track fifteen."

The train was already at the station when they arrived on the platform, so they stepped aboard immediately. They found four seats facing each other and settled into them.

"Where will we sleep?" Gyorgy asked.

"Here," Kati said, indicating the seats. "These will work as beds."

"How long will it take?"

"It will be long, but the trip will be fun." She turned to Adolf. "Do you know how far Vancouver is from here?"

"About five thousand kilometers," he responded. "I think we'll get there in two or three days."

"Wow!" Gyorgy said with a big smile. "That's great!"

When the train pulled out, Kati felt a rush of excitement. They were on the last leg of their long, long journey. Leaning back, she enjoyed watching the countryside rush by. Gyorgy and Judit were also content to look out the window. Within a few hours, both children were lulled to sleep by the gentle rocking of the train. Kati found it hard not to take a nap herself.

As the afternoon rolled by, the conductor informed them that their meals would be covered by the train ticket. When Kati and Adolf entered the dining car with the children, their jaws dropped. Before them were a few dozen tables, each with pressed white linen table cloths.

"Are those flowers real, Mommy?" Gyorgy whispered.

"Yes, darling. I believe they are," she said, marveling at the little vase of small blue buds on their table.

They sat down gingerly, admiring every aspect of the

moving restaurant. Kati tentatively touched the sterling silver fork, running her finger down the handle. When she lifted it, she admired its weight.

When the waiter in black coat-tails made his way to them, she accepted the menu. Working together, they managed to figure out the words. Adolf ordered macaroni and cheese for the children and salmon with vegetables for the two of them. The waiter also brought chocolate milk for the children, which was a rare treat. Gyorgy couldn't stop touching the glass, taking small sips and smacking his lips with delight.

Suddenly, the train lurched to the right and his attention shifted. He cried out in horror as his prized treat spilled all across the pristine white linen table cloth. Kati paled, her eyes flying to Adolf, who looked as horrified as she felt.

"Don't worry, ma'am," the waiter said with a gentle smile, seeming to appear out of nowhere. "It happens more than you can realize."

Before she knew what happened, all traces of the accident were removed and a new white table cloth was laid over the table. Then they ate the most delicious dinner they'd ever had. When they had all finished their dessert, the four went back to their seats, pleasantly full and ready for sleep.

As the children fell asleep curled up in their seats, Kati cuddled in her husband's arms. She knew she'd sleep well that night.

"It's amazing, isn't it?" she said. "Can you believe we're here, on this train? It feels more like a dream."

"Yes, darling. It really is a dream, a dream come true," he answered, kissing her brow gently.

EPILOGUE

SEVERAL DECADES LATER, Kati was visiting her daughter, Judy, in Arizona for the second time that winter. It was nice to escape the harsh winters of Montreal and she always enjoyed spending time with Judy and her family. She was proud of her daughter, now a mother herself and a children's book author.

As they sat on the terrace, each enjoying a cup of coffee, Kati found herself reminiscing about the journey they'd endured to make it out of Hungary so many years prior. Although Judy had no recollection of the experience, she loved the stories nonetheless. As always, they discussed the generous young girl, who had been so instrumental in their escape.

"I bet Annemarie has grandchildren by now," Judy mused.

"As a matter of fact, she does!" Kati replied with a smile. "You know, we lost touch for many years after your father died. Then Annemarie found a way to reconnect with me. Since then, we exchange pictures every Christmas."

"Mother, what do you think of the idea of my sending her a few of my books? I'd also like to write her a little note, expressing my gratitude for all she's done for us. Maybe someone in her family could translate."

Kati reached out to touch her daughter's hand. "I love that idea!"

Several weeks later, Judy received a return email from Annemarie, much to her surprise. Through an online translation program, the two women developed an instant dialogue. Both had many questions for the other and were able to catch up quickly.

As coincidence would have it, Judy had booked a river cruise for later in the year, one that would pass through Vienna. Annemarie was thrilled to learn that she would see her long lost friend.

As Judy packed for the Danube River cruise, she kept the phone receiver balanced between her ear and shoulder. "Mom, I really wish you could join us on this trip."

"I do, too," Kati said with a drawn out sigh. "I just can't travel like that anymore. It's hard for me to admit, but I'm already eighty-seven. Before the latest hip surgery, I was walking better. But the last few years have been difficult."

"I know, Mama."

"I am so happy that you will get to meet Annemarie, though. Give her a hug from me, too."

"I will. Most definitely!"

"Her parents did visit a long time ago. They had come to visit a relative who'd moved to Canada. We were so happy to see them both. Do you remember? You would have been about eight."

"A little," Judy hedged. "Well, no, not really."

"They were such lovely people and we were so happy to see them again."

"Are they still alive?"

"No. Sadly, they passed away."

Judy stopped packing and sat on her bed. "When I planned this cruise, I never dreamed it would be so meaningful. At that time, I hadn't spoken to or even thought it possible to meet Annemarie. And I wish we had considered bringing our son, Andrew. But he's in the middle of exams, anyway. Another time perhaps."

"Do you think she'll be able to show you the church where we met so long ago?" Kati whispered.

"She said she would," Judy replied. "Nathan and I are also planning to see the old apartment in Budapest, down the street from the famous Doheny Synagogue. This trip has turned out to be my *birthright history tour*!"

Both women chuckled then chatted a few more minutes before her mother wished her the best and hung up. Judy finished up all of her last-minute packing and travel tasks before going to sleep. She set her alarm for five o'clock and tried her best to sleep with all the excitement coursing through her.

As the cruise ship began the arrival maneuvers into Vienna, Judy clung to the rail. She was hours away from meeting Annemarie and the excitement was welling up inside her.

What a strange coincidence, she thought. *We're going to meet on a Friday, after dinner, just like that miraculous night so many years ago.* She looked out at the city and tried to imagine how her parents had braved it all on their own with so little to their name, just hope in their hearts.

As a city clock chimed eight, Judy jogged down the gang plank, with her husband, Nathan, just behind her. She immediately recognized Annemarie, who wore a bright red jacket and a huge smile. As she got closer, Judy could see tears streaming down Annemarie's cheeks and she felt her own throat tighten.

"My Judit! My Judit!" Annemarie cried, as she embraced her.

Judy closed her eyes and felt as if she was floating above her body, watching the scene unfold below her. She had dreamed about this moment for so long. And here she was, with the woman who'd helped her family so many decades ago.

Annemarie introduced Judy and Nathan to her husband, Bernard, her daughter, Judit, and her granddaughter, Sara.

"If you'll allow me," Sara said, "I'd like to translate for you and Grandmama."

"That would be wonderful," Judy said with a nod. She turned to Annemarie and said slowly, "Thank you for everything you did for me and my family." Somehow the words didn't seem enough, but they needed to be spoken anyway.

"It was my pleasure," Annemarie replied.

"You know, people toss the words around about how one person can make a difference. Well, you're living proof that that's true!"

"Oh, my Judit!" Annemarie said, squeezing Judy tightly. "I can't believe we're together again. It's like a dream come true!"

They embraced a little longer before Annemarie pulled away and grabbed Judy by the hand. "Come on," she said. "Let's start by sharing a little wine and catch up. I know just the place."

They went to the Sacher Hotel and ordered a bottle of Riesling. Annemarie leaned in and said, "Sara is a local harpist and has arranged a surprise for you tomorrow. She will perform a little concert on your cruise ship in honor of your visit."

"Wow! Thank you so much," Judy whispered. "That's amazing!"

Sara blushed. "It's my pleasure," she said.

Annemarie beamed at Judy. "So, what happened to you after you arrived in Montreal? You went to Vancouver, right?"

"That's right," Judy said, taking a sip of her wine. "You remember my father was determined to find a job. Well, he found work as a salesman in a men's clothing store. Since he spoke several languages, and had such an engaging personality, it didn't take long for him to be snapped up."

"Yes, Adolf was always so charming and sincere," Annemarie said, her eyes shining.

"And he never took *no* for an answer," Judy said with a fond smile. "His favorite expression was always, *There's no such word as can't!*"

"I remember that he lived by that philosophy," Annemarie said. "So, how long did you stay in Vancouver?"

"Just a little less than a year. Mom couldn't stand the constant rain and isolation, so we moved back to Montreal."

"Poor Kati," Annemarie said with a sigh. "It must have been rough."

"Yes, it was, but it was definitely better for her in Montreal. She had friends there who had also arrived from Hungary, so she did not feel so isolated. I really don't know how my parents managed it back then. I mean, they had no family, only a few dollars to their name and two small children to boot."

"I could tell your parents were special people when I met them."

Judy smiled. "Thank you. Piecing things together, Montreal became a good home for us. Mom told me that our friends became our family. And Dad found another job at a men's clothing factory while Mom worked from home to supplement the income."

"What did she do?"

"She mended stockings. It wasn't easy for her, I'll tell you that much. She'd take care of us all day then work in the evening."

Annemarie shook her head. "I've always admired your mother so much. With all that she'd been through, she still had so much love in her heart."

"Yes, she's incredible," Judy said with a nod. "It was only years later, when Dad was able to open his own store, that she could finally quit working."

Annemarie gave a low whistle. "Wow! His own store? That's impressive!"

"Yes, a little place called Three Star Clothing, after his three children."

"That's right, three!" exclaimed Annemarie. "Kati had sent me pictures of you all. Your sister's name is Shirley, right?"

"Yes, she's seven years younger than me. Born in Montreal."

"And how is Gyorgy?"

"He is doing very well, thank you. Can you believe he's married with three children? And recently, he became a grandfather."

"Wow, I can't picture that! I still see him as a little boy. So, it looks like Canada worked out well for you all!"

"It certainly wasn't easy for my parents, but it was always clear to me that us children came first. Growing up, they were so protective of us, cherishing us. I'm eternally grateful for the sacrifices they made to bring us to Canada so many years ago."

Judy and Annemarie continued to talk into the evening, exchanging small gifts and enjoying each other's company. When it started to rain, they paid the bill and hurried to the Metro station. Annemarie stayed close to Judy, sheltering her with her umbrella. Judy smiled up at her, catching a glimpse of how young Annemarie had probably taken care of her as a toddler. So little had changed over the last sixty years.

The next day, after lunch, they met again. True to her word, Annemarie showed Judy all the places her parents had stopped at when they had first arrived in Vienna. Judy wished she could remember more of that night. As it was, all she could do was envision what it might have been like for the three of them to stand outside the Rothschild Center waiting for her father to return.

But when she arrived at the church, she had no trouble picturing her mother meeting the Just family outside on the steps for the first time. Judy gingerly touched the tall wooden doors of the church and closed her eyes.

This was the spot. I know it!

"Do you think we could see the apartment where you lived?" Judy asked.

"Yes, of course."

They walked the kilometer to the apartment building

and were fortunate that someone Annemarie knew buzzed them in. They offered to show Judy what their apartment looked like, since it was so similar to the Just's old place.

As she climbed the stairs, her heart raced as she realized her mother probably touched the same banister, felt the same concrete steps beneath her shoes.

This happened to me, Judy thought, feeling the prick of tears in the back of her eyes. *My family traveled this path to bring us to where we are today.*

When they left the building, Judy felt an even greater appreciation for her family's history than she ever had before. There was nothing that could ever come closer to walking in her parents' footsteps or even her own baby ones.

After Sara's harp concert on the ship, Judy walked Annemarie down the gangplank and embraced her one last time. This new, yet old friend would be remembered forever by Judy and her family. Judy vowed then and there that the generations to come would know of her parents' courage, of the brave choices they had made, and the unforgettable kindness of a young sixteen-year-old girl named Annemarie.

PHOTOGRAPHS

George (Gyorgy) Egett

Judy (Judit) Egett

Kati (Krausz) and Adolf Egett

Annemarie Just, her father
Leopold and her brothers.

Annemarie Just, her mother
Anna and her brother.